D0049065

More Praise for *Source*

"In this breakthrough combination of modern physics and ancient wisdom, Jaworski explains the revolutionary process of knowledge creation and the actualization of hidden potentials that lie dormant in all of us. *Source* is what we have waited for, the guide to a future based on belonging, on compassionate intelligence, and on partnership in the evolution of the universe."
—**Don Wukasch, MD, cardiovascular surgeon (retired), Texas Heart Institute**

"*Source* is an enthralling and enduring gift that profoundly strengthens our belief in ourselves and in each other. Joseph has given us a touchstone of a book to help us realize our significance, influence, and value as individuals and as a united one. Our purpose lies within us, and Joseph's stories help us grasp our nature, our raison d'être—maybe for the first time."
—**Barbara Annis, Chair, Women's Leadership Board, Harvard University's Kennedy School, and CEO and founder, Barbara Annis and Associates, Inc.**

"I am continually amazed at Jaworski's ability to peel back the layers concealing breakthrough solutions to seemingly intractable organizational problems. *Source* reveals that beneath those obstructive layers there exists within individuals the potential to transform their organizations, allowing both to achieve their full potential. Jaworski's contact with brilliant thinkers uniquely equips him to write this truly insightful book."
—**John Cater, President and CEO Emeritus, Compass Bank–Houston**

"When faced with organizational or individual decisions, regardless of our efforts to gather as much data as possible, there is always a gap between the clear-cut facts and the final decision. Jaworski takes us from closing that gap by leaps of faith to doing so with sure faith in our leaps. A must-read for critical change decision-making success."
—**Paul Comstock, Chairman, Paul Comstock Partners**

"Joseph Jaworski has once again demonstrated his most unusual talent at bringing forth a valuable and rare contribution to improving the lives of all of us. While it is obvious that reading the book will certainly improve the performance of all who are charged with decision-making responsibility in any organization, it will also benefit all who follow its suggestions as they face each day."
—**Gibson Gayle, Chairman of the Board, MD Anderson Foundation, and former President, State Bar of Texas**

"Joseph Jaworski has once again demonstrated his most unusual talent at bringing forth a valuable and rare contribution to improving the lives of all of us. While it is obvious that reading the book will certainly improve the performance of all who are charged with decision-making responsibility in any organization, it will also benefit all who follow its suggestions as they face each day."

—**Gibson Gayle, Chairman of the Board, MD Anderson Foundation, and former President, State Bar of Texas**

"*Source* is a fascinating book and a gripping read, particularly for believers in the power of nature and its impact on getting you closer to the Source. Participating in the retreat where Joseph met the mountain cat left a profound impression on me and led to my decision to redirect my career and to follow my heart. I love the concept of generation IV leadership. This is the kind of leader we need to rescue the world."

—**Kees van der Graaf, Executive-in-Residence, IMD, and former Executive Director, Unilever PLC**

SOURCE

also by Joseph Jaworski
Synchronicity: The Inner Path of Leadership

SOURCE

THE INNER PATH
OF KNOWLEDGE CREATION

Joseph Jaworski
Betty Sue Flowers, Editor

Berrett–Koehler Publishers, Inc
San Francisco
a BK Business book

Berrett-Koehler Publishers, Inc.

235 Montgomery Street, Suite 650

San Francisco, CA 94104-2916

Tel: (415) 288-0260 Fax: (415) 362-2512 www.bkconnection.com

Ordering Information

Quantity sales. Special discounts are available on quantity purchases by corporations, associations, and others. For details, contact the "Special Sales Department" at the Berrett-Koehler address above.

Individual sales. Berrett-Koehler publications are available through most bookstores. They can also be ordered directly from Berrett-Koehler: Tel: (800) 929-2929; Fax: (802) 864-7626;

www.bkconnection.com

Orders for college textbook/course adoption use. Please contact Berrett-Koehler: Tel: (800) 929-2929; Fax: (802) 864-7626.

Orders by U.S. trade bookstores and wholesalers. Please contact Ingram Publisher Services,

Tel: (800) 509-4887; Fax: (800) 838-1149; E-mail: customer.service@ingrampublisherservices.com; or visit www.ingrampublisherservices.com/Ordering for details about electronic ordering.

Berrett-Koehler and the BK logo are registered trademarks of Berrett-Koehler Publishers, Inc.

Printed in the United States of America

Berrett-Koehler books are printed on long-lasting acid-free paper. When it is available, we choose paper that has been manufactured by environmentally responsible processes. These may include using trees grown in sustainable forests, incorporating recycled paper, minimizing chlorine in bleaching, or recycling the energy produced at the paper mill.

Library of Congress Cataloging-in-Publication Data

Jaworski, Joseph, 1934–

    Source : the inner path of knowledge creation / Joseph Jaworski ; Betty Sue Flowers, editor. — 1st ed.

    p. cm.

    Includes bibliographical references and index.

    ISBN 978-1-57675-904-2 (hbk. : alk. paper)

    1. Self-realization.   2. Creative ability.   3. Leadership.   4. Success.   5. Entrepreneurship—Psychological aspects.   I. Flowers, Betty Sue.   II. Title.

    BJ1470.J37 2012

    150—dc23   2011039994

First Edition

16 15 14 13 12 11   10 9 8 7 6 5 4 3 2 1

Project management: Lisa Crowder, Adept Content Solutions, LLC, Urbana, IL

Full-service book production: Adept Content Solutions, LLC, Urbana, IL

Jacket design: Cassandra Chu

For my children

Joseph S.

Leon

Shannon

FOUR PRINCIPLES

1. **There is an open and emergent quality to the universe.**
   A group of simple components can suddenly reemerge at a higher
   level of self-organization as a new entity with new properties.
   We can't find a cause or reason for this emergent quality, but as
   we experience it again and again, we see that the universe offers
   infinite possibility.

2. **The universe is a domain of undivided wholeness; both
   the material world and consciousness are parts of the same
   undivided whole.**
   The totality of existence is enfolded within each fragment of
   space and time – whether it is a single object, thought, or event.
   Thus, everything in the universe, including human intentions and
   ways of being, affects everything else, because everything is part of
   the same unbroken whole.

3. **There is a creative Source of infinite potential enfolded in the
   universe.**
   Connection to this Source leads to the emergence of new realities
   – discovery, creation, renewal, and transformation. We are
   partners in the unfolding of the universe.

4. **Humans can learn to draw from the infinite potential of the
   Source by choosing to follow a disciplined path toward self-
   realization and love, the most powerful energy in the universe.**
   The path may include teachings from ancient traditions
   developed over thousands of years, contemplative practices, and
   direct exposure to the generative process of nature.

·

CONTENTS

INTRODUCTION
THE CAPACITY TO SENSE
AND ACTUALIZE EMERGING
FUTURES

IN DISCOVERING OUR OWN PURPOSE AND MEANING, WE ENRICH MEANING IN THE UNIVERSE – WE CREATE SOMETHING OF SIGNIFICANCE THAT HAS NOT BEEN THERE. WE ARE PART OF IT, AND IT IS PART OF US. WE ARE PARTNERS IN THE EVOLUTION OF THE UNIVERSE.

Beginning in 1973, with my country in the throes of a leadership crisis that came to be known as "Watergate" and with my personal life entering its own crisis, I began a journey of discovery that I chronicled in *Synchronicity: The Inner Path of Leadership.*

Soon after the book was published, readers began asking me questions about fundamental aspects of the lessons I had learned from my direct experiences. The truth is, I couldn't answer them. At times, as I would conduct workshops and work in client systems, I felt I was like a lawyer "practicing without a license." There were missing pieces to the "whole" I just couldn't articulate. Sometimes I felt I was coming close to knowing – I was gaining tacit knowledge, but I couldn't give voice to it.

Some of the readers asked me to explore with them the subject of society's belief systems – our internal image of reality. As I later understood, they were asking me about metaphysics, the philosophy of being and knowing. Metaphysics was far beyond anything I had considered up to that moment. All I knew was that what I was describing fit my direct experience – and the direct experience of hundreds of readers who were contacting me saying, "Now I know I'm not crazy."

All of these questions and my own growth eventually led me to embark on a whole new search to understand the fundamental principles underlying these experiences. Ultimately, I came to realize that the drive to learn and know our fundamental nature is a basic human need. Metaphysics formats and enables experience, and, in turn, molds scientific, social, and individual reality. It provides a description of human experience that satisfies a deep longing within us. The mathematician, physicist, and philosopher, H. Dean Brown, in answer to the question, "What is the use of metaphysics?" replied, "We become what we behold."

The futurist Willis Harman once said to me, "By deliberately changing the internal image of reality, people can change the world. Indeed," he added, "the real fundamental changes in societies have come about not from dictates of governments and the results of battles, but through vast numbers of people changing their minds."

Since the publication of the first edition of *Synchronicity*, I've been searching for the principles that lie at the heart of what I described there – the capacity we have to sense and actualize emerging futures and to shape the future instead of simply responding to the forces at large. What is the *source* of our capacity to access the knowledge for action we need in the moment? How can we learn to enable that capacity, individually and collectively?

The answers to these questions were slowly revealed to me over a fifteen-year period. Because I now feel adequate to be explicit about what I've learned, I've written this book: *Source: The Inner Path of Knowledge Creation.* In it, I've attempted not only to tell the story of my quest for the principles that form the basis of my experiences as described in *Synchronicity*, but also to understand the nature of what I have called – for lack of a better term – "the Source," or sometimes, depending on the context, "Source."

By its very nature, the Source cannot be defined. The physicist David Bohm told me that "the reality which is most immediate to us cannot be stated." And Robert Jahn and Brenda Dunne, two scientists whom I interviewed for this book, said:

> . . . there exists a much deeper and more extensive source of
> reality, which is largely insulated from direct human experience,
> representation, or even comprehension. It is a domain that has
> long been posited and contemplated by metaphysicians and
> theologians, Jungian and Jamesian psychologists, philosophers
> of science, and a few contemporary progressive theoretical
> physicists, all struggling to grasp and to represent its essence
> and its function. A variety of provincial labels have been
> applied, such as "Tao," "Qi," "prana," "void," "Akashic record,"
> "Unus Mundi," "unknowable substratum," "terra incognita,"
> "archetypal field," "hidden order," "aboriginal sensible
> muchness," "implicate order," "zero-point vacuum," "ontic (or
> ontological) level," "undivided timeless primordial reality,"
> among many others, none of which fully captures the sublimely
> elusive nature of this domain. In earlier papers we called it the
> "subliminal seed regime," but for our present purposes we shall
> henceforth refer to it as the "Source."

While it cannot be defined, Source can be experienced. The first
time I experienced it was during a tornado I describe in the prologue
to this book. My quest since then has not been for a definition but for
an understanding of how we can have a connection to it – how we can
engage in a deep dialogue with it. Dialogue with the Source leads to the
kind of creativity associated with the most successful entrepreneurial
undertakings. Action based on such "primary knowing" can be
"shockingly effective."

This fifteen-year journey covered a long and winding path during
which a colleague and I were inspired to explore what we later developed
as a "U-process" for accessing emerging futures. The exploration of the
U-theory led to our writing *Presence: An Exploration of Profound Change in
People, Organizations, and Society*.

But the work with the U-process and our thinking about the U-theory
left me dissatisfied. Real transformation, it seemed to me, occurred at
what I began to call "the bottom of the U" and involved something
beyond what we were doing – something we didn't really understand. I
began calling it "the Source." A leader's ability to access this Source often
made the difference between success and failure, as I learned in a painful
way when a large pilot project failed. At this juncture, my road diverged
from that of my colleagues, and I began the journey that has led to this
book.

At the heart of what I discovered during my journey to understand Source are four principles, which I've described preceding this introduction. While I have attempted to state these principles as simply and succinctly as I can, exploring them and how they were developed is part of the story I tell in this book – and truly understanding them deeply will take me the rest of my lifetime.

In the process of this search, I gave serious consideration to the Western scientific-materialistic worldview – our underlying belief system, which has prevailed in the West for over two hundred years. I believe that this belief system is no longer adequate for the issues our society is facing; that an historic shift is now occurring; and that a more comprehensive worldview is emerging. Institutions can play a leading role in enabling this emerging worldview.

At the time *Synchronicity* was published, the most admired institutions were led by what Robert Greenleaf described as "servant leaders." Scott Peck has referred to these as "Stage III" leaders. But I believe that a more advanced generation of institutions must be led by what I call "Stage IV" leaders. Stage IV leaders embody the characteristics and values of servant leaders, but have matured to a more comprehensive and subtle level of development. They exhibit a capacity for extraordinary functioning and performance. At the heart of this kind of performance is a capacity for accessing tacit knowing that can be used for breakthrough thinking, strategy formation, and innovation, including envisioning and creating the kind of institution or society we desire.

Stage IV leaders believe that there is an underlying intelligence within the universe, which is capable of guiding us and preparing us for the futures we must create. They combine their cognitive understanding of the world around them with a strong personal sense of possibility – the possibility of actualizing hidden potentials lying dormant in the universe, a view that carries with it the power to change the world as we know it.

Institutions guided by this quality of leadership, from line leaders to the very top, will, in my view, flourish in the decades to come. Because of their success, these institutions will become living examples of what is possible in the face of accelerating complexity and high turbulence. Operating from this new worldview, these living examples can play a major role in shifting the prevailing belief system.

In discovering our own purpose and meaning – whether of our institutions or of our own personal lives – we enrich meaning in the universe. We create something significant that has not been there. We are part of it, and it is part of us. We are partners in the evolution of the universe.

I hope that *Source* will serve your own path toward higher stages of growth and development – and that it will also serve the leadership of your institution and of society as a whole.

PROLOGUE

You have capacities within you that are phenomenal,
if you only knew how to release them.
  – *David Bohm*

It was Monday, May 11, 1953. I was eighteen years old and a freshman at Baylor University in Waco, Texas, which then had a population of 85,000 people. I was in my dormitory room, alone, completing an essay due later that week. By around 4:30 that afternoon, the sky had turned dark. It had been raining hard for a couple of hours, but now the rain was coming down in sheets, and the wind was picking up. All of a sudden it was as if a hundred freight trains were roaring through my room. It lasted only seconds, but I was stunned. "My God – what was that?" Within minutes the rain subsided to a light drizzle.

Without really thinking, I put on a windbreaker and baseball cap and ventured out. I was not making a deliberate decision to go. I just found myself heading in the direction of downtown, not stopping to assess the risk of walking among all the live electrical lines that were strewn across the streets. There was no one on the streets – no cars – no one in sight.

I passed near Katy Park where the local Texas League baseball team played. The park had essentially disappeared, collapsed in on itself. I could see only one wall standing. I noticed a building nearby that was cut in half, as if by a great meat cleaver. I walked directly up to the center of town, the corner of Fifth and Austin, where the six-story R. T. Dennis Building was located. That was a furniture store that covered most of a city block and was across the corner from Chris's Café, where I often had dinner.

As it turned out, that corner – Fifth and Austin – was the epicenter of a deadly tornado. As I approached the corner, I was astonished to see that the Dennis Building had vanished. In its place was a towering heap of rubble. The vacuum created from the tornado had blown the walls outward, causing all six stories to collapse onto one another, falling into the basement. The walls of bricks had flattened the cars in the street beside the building, and the cars themselves were buried under five-to-six feet of bricks. The café and the Palace Club, the pool hall next door where I had often hung out, had also disappeared. They were just an enormous pile of rubble, fifteen-to-twenty feet high.

I learned later that the destruction I saw was the result of the deadliest tornado in Texas history and one of the ten worst ever recorded in US history. The 300-mile-per-hour winds had left a twenty-three-mile path of destruction, including 114 dead and over 1,200 injured.

⊱─┄◆─○─◆┄─⊰

I was one of the first few people on the scene. There was an eerie silence pervading that corner. The few people who were standing around were stunned, in shock. Within just minutes, about a half dozen of us self-organized into a team and began the first stages of a search-and-rescue effort. A doctor was nearby, helping to guide us. We worked as a team in that particular area through the night and into the midday Tuesday, doing our best to locate and dig out survivors. Within minutes of arriving, I found one person in the rubble. We dug her out, and as I held her in my arms, taking her to the place the doctor was designating as a field hospital, he examined her and quickly said, "She's gone. Let's make this the morgue. Over here will be the field hospital."

It was a delicate operation. We patiently dismantled the debris piece by piece. We worked as a team in that particular area through the night, using flashlights and gloves that had been brought to the scene. The police, using bullhorns, directed everyone not involved in the search and rescue away from the area.

Within an hour or so of my arrival, help from the nearby Connally Air Force Base came. And by 2:30 that morning, heavy equipment had arrived – but where we were working, it was useless, even dangerous. As we found survivors, we had to be exceedingly careful not to allow the debris to shift and crush them. Eventually, we dug out a number of survivors and recovered twenty-nine bodies from the café and pool hall area.

Our little team stayed intact the entire time. While we worked together, I experienced a palpable energy field surrounding us. My sense of awareness was acute. I possessed an uncanny clarity, a sort of panoramic knowing. Time slowed down. We were able to perform very difficult tasks with apparent ease. We would accomplish something so extraordinary, I would "look over my shoulder," so as to speak, and wonder "How in the world did we accomplish that?" Yet in the moment, it seemed so natural. It was almost effortless, yet we were exerting a supreme effort. We operated as a "single intelligence" – as one organism – with exceedingly high coherence.

We self-organized from the very beginning. Leadership on the team shifted seamlessly in the moment, as required. I was acting without conscious awareness or control, doing tasks without the sense that I was personally performing them. It was as if we were being used as instruments to accomplish what we must. But most of all, I was struck by the deeper level of knowing that I embodied. My premonitions were consistently correct. During those hours, we had the strength, courage, endurance, and internal resources we needed.

Only when our task was done did exhaustion begin to set in. It was early Tuesday afternoon, and we all paused to say goodbye. Nothing was said about what we had all experienced – it was not necessary. It was clear that we all felt it. The true trust and connection remained palpable.

⊱─◆─○─◆─⊰

In the days after the tragedy, I took time to reflect on all that I had experienced. At that stage of my development, I barely knew how to think about it at all. At one level, the whole experience seemed dreamlike. But at another level, I was aware that it would deeply inform the rest of my life.

As I grew and developed over the years, my understanding grew as well. That understanding was heightened by similar experiences, enabling me to glimpse the essence of what had occurred in Waco over those few hours. One experience occurred a few years later when my best friend saved my life by picking the front of a jeep up off my chest after an accident. The energy field I had felt after the tornado and the sense of deep connection was present at that time. Other instances occurred among our law firm's teams when we were in the midst of trying a difficult lawsuit, particularly one where our client was the underdog, and we were trying to redress a great injustice.

Over time, the feeling grew within me that I needed to search for *the source* of these kinds of collective experiences and to determine how to have access to them without a crisis – how to harness this phenomenon in organizational settings for the benefit of all society. By the time I had practiced as a litigator for twenty years, the need to learn more grew so present within me and the crisis of leadership in the country seemed so acute that I decided to leave the practice of law.

Two days after leaving my law firm, I met the great physicist, David Bohm, who taught me that there is a creative Source of infinite potential – the "implicate order" – enfolded in the explicate order, or manifest universe. What I learned that day altered my worldview forever, creating the opening for all that occurred afterward. Just a week after meeting Dr. Bohm, I flew to Houston to form the American Leadership Forum.

During the Leadership Forum years, I began to realize there is a deep hunger for the experience of oneness and for being used for something greater than ourselves. I began to understand that being used in this way is what it means to be human. This is why the experience of being part of a team that is acting as one consciousness in relation to something larger than the individual members stands out as a singular moment in people's lives. Some – like me – spend the rest of their lives looking for ways to recapture the *spirit* of that experience. And others – also like me – spend years attempting to understand the nature of that experience. What is the *Source* of our capacity to access the knowledge for action we need at the moment?

This book is the story of my quest to answer that question.

1. THE SOURCE OF THE ENTREPRENEURIAL IMPULSE – THE QUEST BEGINS

WHAT IS THE SOURCE OF THE ENTREPRENEURIAL IMPULSE? WHAT IS THE SOURCE OF OUR CAPACITY TO ACCESS THE KNOWLEDGE FOR ACTION WE NEED AT THE MOMENT?

In the spring of 1998, I was sitting in the back row of a large auditorium in the Shell Learning Center at the Woodlands just north of Houston. Eighteen months earlier, Shell Oil Company (the then-autonomous unit of the Royal Dutch Shell Group of Companies), Texaco, Inc., and Saudi Aramco had announced their intention to form an alliance of all their refining, distribution, and marketing (their "downstream" operations) in the United States. The "Alliance" would be the largest downstream organization in the world, with annual revenues approaching $40 billion. The Alliance hired Generon, a firm I had cofounded, to help develop its senior leadership and to assist in the integration of the units into a cohesive whole.

On that spring day, about 250 senior officers, who were members of the transition team, had gathered for the kickoff of the new venture. The chief operating officer of Texaco, Glenn Tilton, gave the opening remarks. In those remarks, Tilton identified the greatest challenge facing the Alliance – how to compete effectively with the newer and more nimble entrepreneurial downstream operators that had appeared in the marketplace in the last five years.

"We in this room have been operating in major oil companies as 'elephants.' But starting next week, we're going to have to act as 'gazelles'

11

– to become true entrepreneurs – or we won't be in the phone book in five years."

You could have heard a pin drop. Tilton continued, "We've got to rise to the occasion – but, to be honest – I'm not sure how to begin. I'm counting on each of you to help figure this out. We've got our work cut out for us in more ways than we can ever imagine."

In that instant, the question flashed before me: "What is the *Source* of the entrepreneurial impulse? What is the *Source* of our capacity to access the knowledge for action we need at the moment?"

Although I didn't know the answer, I *absolutely knew* there were important hidden implications I would discover if I stayed committed. In that very instant, my energy completely shifted, as if an internal rheostat had been turned up to the maximum.

I had an utter lack of self-concern, a sense of complete freedom, and a sense of overwhelming urgency. Nothing else mattered to me but to follow this opening, even if I didn't fully understand why.

And that's what I did for the next ten years.

2. A DEEPER REGION OF CONSCIOUSNESS

FOR THE BIG DECISIONS IN LIFE, YOU NEED TO REACH A DEEPER REGION OF CONSCIOUSNESS. MAKING DECISIONS THEN BECOMES NOT SO MUCH ABOUT 'DECIDING' AS ABOUT LETTING AN INNER WISDOM EMERGE.
– Brian Arthur

As the session broke up, I found the chief learning officer, Gary Jusela, and, over a three-hour lunch, described to him the opening I saw – to develop a process whereby teams could sense the way the future wants to unfold, and to enable that unfolding. I felt that teams could guide this process by their intention, their way of being, and their choices. I told him we would be on a search for the process by which transformational breakthroughs in any field occur, the creation of knowledge that changes the world as we know it. Gary instantly understood what I was talking about.

The next morning, we went to see Jim Morgan, the joint CEO of the Alliance. I reminded Jim of Tilton's remarks and of the challenges he had laid down to the senior leaders. I said, "Jim, I can help you develop the *entrepreneurial impulse* in your people. I need eight months to finish the research, develop the process, and run a pilot. We can create a leadership laboratory, a learning environment that can help these managers 'act like gazelles,' enabling them to create significant new growth platforms for the Alliance and to significantly improve their operational performance." Right there, on the spot, Jim gave Gary and me the green light.

The following day, I flew home to Boston and hired C. Otto Scharmer, who was studying with Peter Senge, with whom I was working at the

MIT Organizational Learning Center, recently reorganized and named The Society of Organizational Learning (SoL). In designing the research agenda, Otto and I decided to seek out and interview at least fifty of the most remarkable thinkers and practitioners in the field of innovation, discovery, high performance, and entrepreneurship. We agreed it would be my responsibility to tap the network I had been building since my founding of the American Leadership Forum at the beginning of the 1980s.

That same week, I developed a list of the first twenty people we would see. At the top of the list was Srikumar Rao, who conceived the pioneering course at Columbia Business School, "Creativity and Personal Mastery," and Michael Ray, Professor of Creativity and Innovation at Stanford University's Graduate School of Business. Another was a noted psychologist, Michael Lipson, Chief Psychologist at the College of Physicians and Surgeons of Columbia University, who had recently been designated by the family of Abraham Maslow to be his authorized biographer and in the process had been given sole access to Maslow's personal diaries.

Late one night at the office, I created the prioritized list. When I had finished, I packed my briefcase and was on my way out the door when I glanced over at a table in the hallway and noticed a magazine. Its title read *Fast Company*. On pure impulse, I picked it up and flipped it open. There was a sidebar article about a brief conversation the editor Anna Muoio had had with W. Brian Arthur, a pioneer of the new science of complexity. Arthur had also played an instrumental role in establishing the Santa Fe Institute in 1987, when he was teaching at Stanford. The institute was founded by several of the major figures of twentieth-century science, including Kenneth Arrow (economics), Murray Gell-Mann (physics), and Phillip Anderson (physics), all Nobel laureates, along with George A. Cowan, the former head of research at Los Alamos who had worked in the bomb laboratory until, at age sixty-three, he set out to forge "the sciences of the twenty-first century." In Arthur's own words, the mission of the Santa Fe Institute was for science as a whole to achieve a kind of "redemption and rebirth." Brian was invited by Arrow and Anderson to be the first director of the interdisciplinary economics program at the institute in 1988.

The article in *Fast Company* recounted Arthur's early training in operations research, which is a highly scientific, mathematical method of strategy formation and decision making. "I once thought," Arthur was quoted as saying, "that I could make any decisions, whether professional or personal, by using decision trees, game theory, and optimization. Over time, I've changed my mind."

Arthur said that for the day-to-day work of running a business – scheduling a fleet of oil tankers, choosing where to open a new factory – scientific decision theory works pretty well. But "for the big decisions in life, you need to reach a deeper region of consciousness. Making decisions then becomes not so much about 'deciding' as about letting an *inner wisdom* emerge." [Emphasis added.] He concluded the interview by noting, "This approach to decision making requires time, patience, and another key ingredient: courage. It takes courage to listen to your inner wisdom. But once you hear that wisdom, making a decision becomes fairly easy."

The words "deeper region of consciousness" and "inner wisdom" leapt out at me. Brian Arthur had rocketed to the very top of my list. In that moment, I knew that I needed to start with the Santa Fe Institute and proceed from there.

3. BIRTH OF THE U-THEORY

*IN A SENSE, THERE IS NO DECISION-MAKING. WHAT YOU DO JUST BECOMES
OBVIOUS. A TOTALLY DIFFERENT SET OF RULES APPLIES.*

– Brian Arthur

A week later, Otto and I were in New York, seeing Professor Rao
and Dr. Lipson, and the following week, we were in Palo Alto, meeting
with Professor Ray. We were in a car near Menlo Park when my business
partner, Susan Taylor, called me. She had located Brian Arthur at Xerox
PARC and learned that he was writing a book and wasn't taking any
meetings. Susan informed me that I was going to have to call Brian
directly.

I called immediately and managed to get through to him, introducing
myself and explaining our project. When I said that we needed two hours
of his time for an interview, he politely declined, explaining he was
working on a new book and wasn't taking appointments. I pressed him,
telling him of the others who had agreed to see us. There was silence on
the other end for a moment – then he said, "Okay, you can come by this
afternoon for a couple of hours at two o'clock."

I immediately called Gary Jusela and told him of the importance of
this meeting. To this day, I don't completely understand why I did that,
except to say I was operating spontaneously from a deeper source, without
conscious thought or control.

Gary, to his credit, said, "If it's that important, I'm going to be there.
Postpone the meeting until tomorrow morning. I'll catch the red-eye and
meet you at Xerox PARC."

That next morning, Dr. Arthur was extremely cordial. He introduced
us to John Seely Brown, the director of Xerox PARC, showed us all

around, and took us to the large conference room. We set up the recorder and explained to Dr. Arthur that I would lead the interview.

He settled back in his chair and said, "Good. Now, what can I tell you about increasing returns?"

I hesitated for a moment and said, "No, Dr. Arthur. We're here to talk about the source of the entrepreneurial impulse – how to sense and actualize emerging futures." I showed him the *Fast Company* article and said, "This is what led us to you."

He glanced at it, and then there was a long silence in the room. He grew quiet. Finally, Arthur said, "This is not what I expected – it's going to take much longer than we had planned." He then asked us to be extremely protective of the audiotape – that this conversation would involve personal reflections he had shared with no one else.

From that moment, the atmosphere in the conference room shifted in an unmistakable way. We were together in dialogue with Arthur almost five hours, and over this time, the energy field became palpable, just as it had during the crisis in Waco. I felt completely connected to Arthur, as if we were joined together by the same umbilical cord.

Since that day, Brian Arthur and I have spoken about this phenomenon many times, even using the word "sacred" – a time when all of us felt deeply committed to one another in a singular way. It was as if we were acting together as agents to deliver important new knowledge into the world. For me, it was the fulfillment of the promise I had made in the back of the auditorium at the Woodlands – an important moment in a decade-long journey that ended with the writing of this book, *Source*.

Then Arthur began to outline the *process* for tapping into this source – what he called "knowing." He said, "This inner knowing comes from here," pointing to his heart. "In a sense, there is no decision making," he said. "What you do just becomes obvious. A totally different set of rules applies. You hang back. You're more like a surfer or a really good racecar driver. You don't act out of deduction, you act out of an inner feeling; you're not even thinking."

Arthur described the process to us in unmistakable terms, explaining that it entails three major stages or "elements." The first thing you do, he said, is "observe, observe, observe." This kind of intense observation "might take days, or hours, or fractions of a second as in martial arts or sports"; then you "reflect and retreat – allow the inner knowing to emerge." Finally, he said, you "act swiftly, with a natural flow."

The conversation around each of these three elements went deeper and deeper as the hours passed. There were long periods of silence where we all four sat absorbed in the moment – experiencing the depth of the field surrounding us. We were communicating on a different plane. It was unmistakable, powerful, and deeply moving.

Arthur spent a good part of the final two hours of our dialogue describing in great detail the daily work he did with his Taoist teacher in Hong Kong from 1988 to 1992. He went back and forth to Hong Kong during those years, learning and perfecting the practices that helped him gain access to that "place of deeper knowing." He had then returned to his home in northern California and continued his study with the pioneering ecologist, explorer, and educator, John Milton. Milton himself had trained for decades with Tibetan Buddhist and Taoist masters. As it turned out, both Arthur and John became two of my closest friends and guides, and both played key roles in my life in the following years.

The dialogue at Xerox PARC ended with my committing to reconnect with Brian as soon as reasonably possible.

When we walked from the building and got into our car, we all three sat in silence. I was in the driver's seat, and finally looked to Otto who sat next to me. "This is the Holy Grail," I said. "Brian just gave us the very essence of what we've been seeking!"

Brian Arthur's U-Process

Observe
Observe
Observe

Act Swiftly
in Flow

Go to That Place of Deeper Knowing

Then with a sense of high excitement, Otto pulled a tablet from his briefcase and said, "Look – we can model Brian's three elements along a 'U.'"

We drew the first U-process model right there in the parking lot of Xerox PARC, a three-stage sequence around a big "U" on the tablet. On the left side of the U, we wrote "Observe, observe, observe." At the bottom of the U, we wrote "Go to that place of deeper knowing." And on the right side of the U: "Act swiftly in flow."

And with that, we had a preliminary understanding of the core process we had promised Jim Morgan – a process by which transformational breakthroughs in any field occur, the creation of knowledge that changes the world as we know it.

4. A LABORATORY FOR
CREATIVE DISCOVERY

THESE PAST TWO YEARS WE COULDN'T MAKE A WRONG DECISION. IT WAS
EFFORTLESS. OUR PREMONITIONS WERE CONSISTENTLY CORRECT.
– Gary Wilson

We had allotted four months for the interview and research phase of
the project. With the U-process Brian had shared with us, the balance
of the interview phase flew by. During these months collaborating with
Gary and his deputies, we created a design team consisting of managers
from key business units across the Alliance. Meeting with the design
team regularly over several weeks, we cocreated the learning process
for the project. This was seen as an *Action Learning* program, engaging
operating people, working on real Alliance issues in real time. The design
team named the program "The Leadership Lab for Competing in the
Digital Economy." In the Alliance, it became known simply as the "Lab."
Twenty-three managers from twenty-one business units were selected
to participate in this Innovation Lab. These managers represented a
microcosm of the whole system.

In a memo to those selected for the Lab, the design team said that
they saw the Lab as an opportunity to "create a new paradigm for
executive learning." It was designed to "model the concept of leader as
teacher" and "leverage the learning of the twenty-three participants to all
fourteen thousand employees, through acting as role models and creating
subsequent living examples of profound innovation and change in their
respective business units."

The Innovation Lab enabled the team to create and propose new
growth platforms for the Alliance, and, of equal importance, to develop

21

the team's skills to unleash and engage the full creative potential of their respective business units.

One refinery, for example, went "from worst to first" among the eighteen refineries in the Alliance. The refinery was losing, on average, $20 million annually and within two years, swung to a $38-million profit, directly due to people's performance, not market fluctuations.

Gary Wilson, the deputy manager of the refinery, attributed his capacity to lead this transformation to the principles and processes he learned during the Lab experience. Referring to Brian Arthur's process for reaching a "deeper region of consciousness" and "letting an inner wisdom emerge," Wilson told me, "These past two years we couldn't make a wrong decision. It was effortless. Our premonitions were consistently correct."

Another participant, Dave Chapman, accepted the position as CEO of an Alliance business, Lease Trading, which had been underperforming for years and was to be sold. Instead, Chapman grew the business from a gross margin of $20 million to one of $60 million in three years, and he told me that this amazing growth was "as a direct result of understanding the power of and applying the U-process."

After the Innovation Lab was concluded, Otto and I took stock of all that had occurred. We realized we had uncovered a process that could be enormously powerful, with implications not only for business applications, but for society as a whole. We decided that an important next step would be to publish our findings. We had documented all of our interviews, and a report had been prepared by the Shell facilitation team for internal publication. So at that moment, we started preparing a monograph, which ultimately became known within Generon simply as *The Red Book*. *The Red Book* has served as my guide, my "bible" over the ensuing years, as I've worked with the U-process.

5. THE RED BOOK

LEADERS HAVE TO DEVELOP A NEW COGNITIVE CAPABILITY – THE CAPACITY TO
SENSE AND ACTUALIZE EMERGING FUTURES.
– *The Red Book*

The Red Book was written early in May 2000, just after the Alliance
Lab had concluded. It is the first published paper documenting the
uncovering and development of the U-process. Writing this paper, like
conducting the interview process and leading the first Lab, was a time
of enormous excitement and opening for me. The very fact of gathering,
organizing, and documenting the essence of our work over the past year
was an act of deep devotion.

During the entire design process, after the meeting with Brian at
Xerox PARC, Otto and I must have had a hundred conversations in
coffee houses all over the country as we completed our interviews. During
those hours of conversation, we would remain in deep dialogue about
every word that would be inserted around the U figure; the guiding
principles behind each element of the U; and what the process as a whole
could mean for society. We considered the implications for leadership
generally and for organizational leadership in particular.

Throughout those months, we spoke often of the lessons learned
and chronicled in *Synchronicity*; how those lessons about sensing and
actualizing emerging futures provided a foundation for our current work;
and how we had, in fact, been living that very process while uncovering
the balance of the knowledge needed to complete the circle. In these
conversations, the field present during the dialogue with Brian was also
present with us and enabled us to continue to learn at a deeper level. We
were living the process as we created it.

We saw we were helping to give birth to something fragile and new, something that must be nurtured and cared for from the depths of our being. I recalled what I had learned from Erich Fromm in *The Art of Loving* about the elements of love: care, which is the active concern for the life and development of the one we love; responsibility, which is the caring for the loved one's physical needs as well as the loved one's higher needs; and respect, which is allowing the loved one to grow as they need to, on their own terms. Above all, to love this way must be our *supreme concern*. I prayed that I would always devote this quality of concern for what we were being asked to develop and grow.

It was in this state of intensely focused creativity that we wrote *The Red Book*. It took only a week to draft. In its final form, the paper is about fifty pages long. As I look back over what we wrote ten years ago, I see we were, ourselves, sensing the vital nature of the gift we had been given:

> We live in a time of profound change. Leaders across the globe are wrestling with similar challenges in a world that is . becoming increasingly unfamiliar. In order to succeed in such an environment, leaders have to develop a new cognitive capability – the capacity to sense and actualize emerging futures. This capacity constitutes a new form of knowledge creation. For organizations, it also poses a fundamental question: How can this capacity be reliably reproduced or applied, particularly in larger organizations and institutions . . . ? The answer to this question will constitute *the core process around which organizations, industries, and institutions will organize their activities in the future*.

At the same time, we acknowledged that many mysteries surrounded the whole process. Chief among them, for me, was: *What happens at the "bottom" of the U?*

> We hardly know how to begin to describe this process, to give voice to its essence. In what domain does it reside? Is it simply about knowledge creation? Is it about the formation of awareness and will? Is it about mobilizing collective energy, will, and action? Is it all of these? What are the fundamental activities and stages of the process? And what are the qualities that enable this process to take place? The more we probe into the deeper questions of leadership in the context of the emerging new world, the more we realize how little we really know, in terms of *actionable* knowledge.

We acknowledged that the paper represented only a first effort to respond to an enormously important and complex set of questions, that we were exploring vast frontiers of human knowledge, and that whatever we said in the paper was only a beginning. We said, however, that we believed we had identified at least some of the critical components that would represent an answer to at least some of these questions.

We also wrote that we believed the essence of the new leadership would involve building three types of organizational spaces outlined in the design of the laboratory. These spaces enable entrepreneurial leaders to move through all three stages of *observing* (connecting to the world outside), *going to that place of deeper knowing* (connecting to the world within), and *enacting* (bringing forth new ventures and new realities) as aspects of a single core process of large-scale innovation and change.

We concluded:

> In moving through these three spaces and stages, leaders and communities of leaders become the vehicle and conduit through which this emerging new dynamic becomes reality. This is the way true innovators have always worked. Placing these principles and processes at the heart of organizing in the future would revolutionize business, social architectures, and society as a whole.

It would be over eight years later, after three experiments applying the process at scale, that I would begin to understand how delicate the process actually was – and how much hard work, sacrifice, and selflessness were required to enable a team to reliably deliver on its promise. I did not yet understand the *depth* of preparation required for those leading and participating in the process.

Soon after completing *The Red Book*, we decided to hold a "salon" – a three-day dialogue to explore the implications of all we had uncovered and to consider next steps. Peter Senge and Otto had been involved in a global interview project with twenty-five "Thinkers of Knowledge and Leadership" sponsored jointly by McKinsey & Company and SoL. Our Alliance interview project overlapped and dovetailed with the McKinsey/ SoL project. Peter and Otto shared the progress of their project regularly with Michael Jung and Jonathan Day, the two McKinsey partners acting as sponsors for their project and who, themselves, were in the midst of exploring the further reaches of generative leadership. This salon would be a perfect opportunity to learn from them and to establish guiding principles, or "rules for the road," for the next stage of development of the U-process – employing it in more diverse applications.

In addition to the two McKinsey partners, we decided to invite Brian Arthur and Ikujiro Nonaka, whom Otto had interviewed earlier, to the salon. Nonaka was highly respected within US management circles. His work first became known through an influential *Harvard Business Review* article titled "The New Product Development Game," coauthored with Hirotaka Takeuchi, who is dean emeritus of the Graduate School of International Corporate Strategy at Hitotsubashi University and a professor at Harvard Business School.

The article, Nonaka's first to explore organizational knowledge creation, was followed in 1991 with another Takeuchi-coauthored *HBR* article, "The Knowledge-Creating Company." Their 1995 book, *The Knowledge-Creating Company: How Japanese Companies Create the Dynamics of Innovation*, laid out a comprehensive theory of the development of collective intellectual capability. By 2000, Nonaka was becoming known as "the father of knowledge management." His research over the years had opened up an entirely new field that intersected directly with all that I had been exploring since the establishment of the American Leadership Forum in the 1980s.

As it turned out, these three days with Brian and Nonaka were instrumental in my subsequent resolutions of many of the remaining mysteries surrounding the U. During one of the breaks, Nonaka and I had a long conversation about his work, particularly his notions of *tacit knowing*, based on the work of a highly respected physical chemist and philosopher, Michael Polanyi, who argued that human beings create breakthrough knowledge through what he called "indwelling," resulting in sudden illumination.

That conversation planted the seeds that – along with the help of my partner, Kazimierz (Kaz) Gozdz – enabled my later understanding of the enigma lying at the bottom of the U.

Although I didn't know it at the time, the salon also marked the beginning of the divergence of my work from Otto's – ironically, because of a transcript of an interview Otto had conducted with Eleanor Rosch, a professor of cognitive psychology at the University of California in Berkeley and coauthor, along with Francisco Varela and Evan Thompson, of *The Embodied Mind: Cognitive Science and Human Experience*. I began to read Rosch's work and discovered that what she calls "primary knowing" was a profound description of experiencing connection with the Source at the bottom of the U.

Rosch said that primary knowing arises "by means of interconnected wholes (rather than isolated contingent parts) and by means of timeless, direct presentation (rather than through stored representations):

> Such knowing is "open" rather than determinate; and a sense
> of unconditional value, rather than conditional usefulness,
> is an inherent part of the act of knowing itself. Action from
> awareness is claimed to be spontaneous, rather than the result
> of decision making; it is compassionate since it is based on
> wholes larger than the self; and it can be shockingly effective.

From that moment, I was consumed with a passion to explore what I began to call "the bottom of the U" while Otto began his development of what he called "Theory U." It was this passion that led me to open the salon by telling about the Waco tornado and all the other experiences of dialogue with what I now call "the Source."

⊱⭑⭑⊙⭑⭑⊰

At dinner that first night of the salon, just as I sat down next to Brian, he turned to me and said, "You need to come to Baja, Mexico, in February to join John Milton and me on a two-week Sacred Passage." His words were not so much an inquiry or invitation as an instruction.

Years later, Brian told me he had been surprised to hear himself saying this – that his "invitation" came out of nowhere, without conscious forethought or even without the sense of "me" doing it. I had a similar experience in response – without even thinking or checking my calendar, I replied, "I'll be there."

Those two weeks in Baja changed my life.

6. BAJA: THE BIRTH OF
THE GLOBAL LEADERSHIP
INITIATIVE

TOGETHER — WORKING FROM THAT "PLACE OF DEEPER KNOWING" — WE CAN BEGIN TO ADDRESS THE MAJOR PROBLEMS OF OUR TIME.

The first four days and the final two days of the Sacred Passage with John Milton were spent in awareness training at the base camp with a half-dozen other participants, including Brian. We would begin early every morning and work through until dinner time, alternating between formal teaching sessions sitting around a beautifully carved log table under a large palm hut, or *palapa*, and practice sessions in the garden next to the palapa.

The focus of the training was on six core sacred principles John had learned over decades of study with Taoist masters and refined by subsequent study with teachers and mentors from many different traditions representing the world's most respected ancient lineages. John possessed a remarkable capacity to translate this wisdom into highly accessible language and daily practices.

By this time, Brian had studied with John about ten years and had participated in over twenty such passages, some lasting a month or more. Brian acted as my personal coach and guide during the days of training.

The work in the garden consisted of learning to cultivate universal energy through the ancient Chinese practice of qigong. This practice is based on the ancient Chinese medical theory of *qi* (pronounced "chee"), which is seen as the life force (core energy) that animates all living beings. We learned core energy practices which, combined with

29

meditation and other practices in nature, are designed to help prepare us to gain access to the "deeper knowing" Brian spoke to us about at Xerox PARC. In John's words, these disciplines, practiced with commitment and high intention, release the immense possibilities we each hold as human beings.

At the conclusion of the awareness training, as I was departing for the trailhead with my backpack, John put his hand around my forearm, looked me straight in the eye, and said, "Remember, Joe, give your deepest appreciation to nature, and you will be amazed what she will teach you."

I followed all of John's instructions, and during the seven-day solo had a profound encounter with two gray whales. In January and February each year, Baja is teeming with pods of grays. They migrate south every winter from the Bering Sea to the warm lagoons of Baja to breed and calve, a journey of six thousand miles – one of the most extraordinary animal achievements on record.

The area John had designated for our solos was the southernmost extension of the Sonoran desert. A desert mountain range is nearby, extending from the interior right up to the coast. I pitched my tent on a cliff about fifty feet above the ocean on a stretch of vast, unsettled coastline. This place has the striking quality of mountains, desert, and ocean, all merging together. There the beachfront drops abruptly and steeply to the ocean floor – over a hundred meters deep. The configuration creates massive and powerful waves that hammer the coast so fiercely that you can feel the reverberations up to a mile inland. There the whales can come and play in the sea, close to the shore. During my solo, they came within twenty-five meters of my solo site.

On the sixth day of my solo, as I stood on the end of a nearby high bluff facing the ocean, just in front of me, two enormous whales rose into the air seventeen times in perfect unison, their bodies arching completely out of the water, like porpoises, and diving back into the water headfirst.

Then, moments later, from the depths of the ocean, like missiles going straight up into the air, the whales shot up out of the water. Their tails cleared the water, and they hung in the air momentarily, then slipped back straight into the water, seemingly without a ripple. They did this three times.

I was in profound communion with those whales. I had a sense that their state of being surpassed anything I had experienced before. From that moment, my life was different. I was left with a memory of having been in the presence of the divine. The foundations of my identity were shifting again, just as they had when I was in the back of the auditorium at the Woodlands. Sitting on that high bluff, a sudden impulse arose within me. A thought cascaded out of me in an instant: "We need to test the efficacy of the U-process at scale." I realized that just as with the Alliance, we could use the process to develop leaders – only this time, not only from business, but also from government and nongovernmental organizations, who could learn to work together to resolve the most pressing regional and global issues facing humanity. None of these sectors alone can resolve such major issues, but together, working from that "place of deeper knowing," we can begin to address the major problems of our time.

This sudden intuition set me on a path that led to the founding of the Global Leadership Initiative whose purpose was to launch demonstration projects designed to test the U-process at significant scale.

7. DEMONSTRATION PROJECTS

WHAT IS LACKING IS ANY WAY FOR ALL OF THESE GROUPS TO THINK TOGETHER ON BEHALF OF THE LONG TERM AND THEIR COMMON INTERESTS.
– Hal Hamilton

At the conclusion of the solo and the following awareness training, I met with John and Brian to share my insight. We talked for several hours and then agreed to meet the following August at John's place in Crestone, Colorado.

That August, John, Brian, and several of our colleagues from Generon and MIT crystallized the vision to undertake a global and regional effort dedicated to the testing and developing of the U-process as an advanced method for multi-stakeholder problem-solving and leadership development. We all felt a high sense of urgency. And the destruction of the twin towers at the World Trade Center just ten days later served to deepen our commitment. The formal organizing meeting for the initiative took place in New York City, less than a half mile from Ground Zero, exactly thirty days after the towers went down.

Through our network of associates, we began with a round of deep dialogue interviews in seven regions worldwide – our way of "observing" globally to gain insights about which projects to target. We spoke with leaders from multinational business, national governments, multilateral institutions, and civil society as well as from activist organizations from across the Americas, Europe, Africa, and Asia.

I devoted most of my effort during the start-up to raising capital and enrolling key sponsors. While in Europe, I received an invitation to a small gathering in Putten, a tiny village near Amsterdam. That invitation proved to be pivotal to the launch of our two largest demonstration projects because of a man I met there – Antony Burgmans, the chairman of the Anglo-Dutch food giant, Unilever, who later introduced me to a senior Unilever manager, Andre van Heemstra. Andre eventually became a key sponsor of one of the projects, and Antony's company ended up supporting both.

The initiative was formally inaugurated at a meeting at the Trapp Family Lodge in Northern Vermont. For three days, under a tent in a beautiful meadow, seventy people from eleven countries began planning. And six months later, Unilever and Oxfam launched the Sustainable Food Lab (SFL), our first experiment. They were joined by over thirty multinational food companies and nongovernment organizations, major foundations, and government representatives from the United States, the Netherlands, the European Commission, and Brazil. The objective of the undertaking was to "foster collaborative learning across the food supply chain" between Europe, Brazil, and the United States.

At the first organizational meeting of the SFL, the founding participants described the global food system – growing, harvesting, buying, and distributing food – as a classic case of a system largely out of control. They acknowledged that the leaders of those in the system were trying to make the best decisions possible, but they were doing so in a system that is critically fragmented. In their words, they were trapped in a "race to the bottom," going faster and faster toward a destination no one wanted to reach. The codirector of the SFL, Hal Hamilton, described the situation to us this way:

> Most companies think the answer is to use technology to increase productivity. On the other side of the street, many activists are dedicated to fighting big corporations that they see as destroying local farming communities and ecologies. Governments get caught in the middle between corporate pressures to boost production and the political instability of farmers displaced from their lands by falling prices. Rich country governments respond by spending $500 billion a year for farm subsidies, but poor governments don't have this option. What is lacking is any way for all of these groups to think together on behalf of the long term and their common interests.

The founding participants dedicated their efforts to learning how to shift the forces driving these global supply chains in order to ensure a more sustainable future for society worldwide.

Within four years of that organizing meeting, over seventy businesses, governments, farm groups, and nongovernmental organizations joined the Lab. Opportunities were created to incubate innovations at every stage along the entire supply chain. The SFL is now an independent venture, housed at the Sustainability Institute in southern Vermont. Among its achievements is the establishment of a Global Business Coalition for Sustainable Food, which is developing sustainability standards for members worldwide.

In early 2003, we began organizing the second demonstration project, the Partnership for Child Nutrition (PCN). The PCN was initiated by the head of the Unilever foods business in Asia, Tex Gunning. Tex was known throughout Unilever for his leading initiatives that connected his units deeply to one another and to their collective purpose. His work has been chronicled in a book, *To the Desert and Back: The Story of the Most Dramatic Business Transformation on Record.*

Tex and I had first met in Helsinki, where we had made a joint presentation at the first Global Forum for SoL. After our presentation, Tex told me he had been deeply moved over the prior two years by the suffering of malnourished children in India, where one of Unilever's largest operating companies, Hindustan-Lever Limited, was located. The story he told me was stunning. Over 46 percent of children in India suffer from malnutrition, a rate higher than sub-Saharan Africa. An estimated 75 million of India's children from birth to three years old are undernourished, the root cause of a high level of many preventable diseases and of impaired development. Despite the country's many advances, Tex explained that the scope and persistence of malnutrition in India has remained a major obstacle to the country's economic growth and development.

Tex had looked into the matter and concluded that the cause was a systemic breakdown operating across all sectors. He wanted to find breakthrough solutions to the problem and believed that to do so would require engaging all sectors – government, nongovernmental organizations, hospitals, research institutions, academia, villages, and mothers. He felt the Lab process could provide a path to a solution. He understood, based on what I had told him of our experience in the Food Lab, that enacting a new system is not about getting "the answer," but about developing deeply connected networks of engaged and trusting people who are guided by a common understanding of the current systems and a deep commitment to create new systems.

A month later, I was in Rotterdam meeting with Antony and his Unilever executive team as well as many of Unilever's senior managers. Over the next ten days, we gained the full support of Unilever's senior management to undertake the project. Antony and Tex told me of Unilever's strong ties to the Indian government through its well-regarded subsidiary. The company also had a good emerging relationship with the United Nations Children's Fund (UNICEF), who they thought could be an important local supporter of the initiative through its country's program and its national committee in India. The missing partner was an NGO with a strong reputation in India and access to civil society organizations committed to reducing child malnutrition. That partner turned out to be the Synergos Institute, a well-regarded NGO in New York with strong ties to India.

The PCN created the Bhavishya Alliance ("Bhavishya" is Sanskrit for "future"), an unprecedented coalition of Indian corporations, government agencies, and civil society organizations with a commitment to halve the rate of child malnutrition in India – especially for children zero-to-three years old – by 2015. The partnership focused first on the state of Maharashtra, where an integrated set of initiatives was implemented. Phase I, which ran through 2008, covered five rural districts and one ward in Mumbai. The total population in that project area is an estimated 2.2 million people, with 40,000 undernourished children.

Phase II, started in 2009, covers a project area of five rural districts with an estimated population of 19 million, and seven additional vulnerable wards in Mumbai. The partnership is now exploring options for child nutrition projects in countries beyond India, particularly in Africa, where the rate of child malnutrition remains intractably high.

><·>·O·<·><

A third demonstration project was created in the Northern Great Plains region (North Dakota, South Dakota, Nebraska, Indiana, and

Minnesota) by a half dozen business and community leaders led by Jerry Nagel of North Dakota. These people gathered together over the course of several months and identified core issues facing the region, believing that some way must be found to address deep systemic issues, including accelerated migration of rural youth to urban centers outside the region; severe racial divisions preventing the region's Native American and Latino populations from contributing their full potential to the region; hidden and insidious poverty trapping families in a paycheck-to-paycheck existence and a dependence on federal or state programs for survival; and growing drug and violence problems, particularly in rural communities, caused by isolation and despair. They concluded:

> If the region is to reach its fullest economic, social, environmental, and spiritual potential, it can no longer seek solutions to these societal concerns through the old paradigm of technical solutions. Restructuring or re-engineering strategies and reframing or rethinking our mental models is no longer sufficient. The solutions to these systemic problems lie at a much deeper level. We must also develop the collective will and spirit to change our beliefs and habits. To do this requires shared conversations, an open mind and heart, and thinking and creativity at a much deeper level than we have been willing to undertake in the past.

>-+-4>-0-<+-+-<

In 2004, the coalition of leaders decided to initiate a U-Process Innovation Lab with the declared purpose of "creating a team of committed current and emerging leaders who care deeply about the economic, social and environmental future of the Northern Great Plains to work together to cause long-term systemic change in the region." A team of twenty-nine participants was chosen, "representing a microcosm of the regions' social system, including representatives from agriculture, youth, education, manufacturing, government, finance, the arts, urban and suburban areas, conventional and alternative energy, community activists, immigrant populations, the faith community, philanthropists, and transportation." Every team member committed a full thirty days to the Lab over two years. The design of the Lab mirrored that used in the Alliance and the other two demonstrations projects.

The Lab ended in late 2007, resulting in the establishment of The Meadowlark Institute as an incubator to provide "living examples of systemic change and through these demonstrated examples create a vision of the Northern Great Plains as a place of opportunity for all people." The Institute's mission statement declares:

> A core belief of the Institute is that the necessary resources to solve our problems and create our futures are already present within us and the challenge is for us to work together to bring our individual and collective knowledge, intelligence, wisdom, creativity, and inner courage into play.

The Meadowlark Institute was named after the Western meadowlark, a bird whose "cheerful song is often described as inspiring and is seen as an announcement of the arrival of spring. The bird is often associated with hope and renewal."

The Institute is active in the region, providing strategic planning, leadership training and development, team building, and civic engagement services to businesses, civic organizations, and local communities throughout the Great Plains region.

8. THE MOUNTAIN LION

WHEN THE MOUNTAIN LION SHOWS UP, THERE IS A CHOICE TO BE MADE.

In late July 2006, a number of Generon colleagues and I were coleading a retreat in Montana for the Global Philanthropy Circle (GPC) founded by Peggy Dulaney, the chair of Synergos, and her father, David Rockefeller. GPC is a network of leading philanthropic families from across the world, committed to using their time, influence, and resources to fight global poverty and social injustice.

It had been a spectacular spring and summer that year in Montana – there was a profusion of wildflowers up where I was on solo for four days and three nights. My site was located just under Black Butte at 9,800 feet. There was a clear mountain stream originating out of the rock formation just under the butte, and the wildflowers were waist high all around the headwaters of the stream.

There were over forty species of flowers represented on the mountain that summer, Peggy told me. It seemed that all were there with me. The most predominant were the fuchsia bells – they were in profusion just beside the water. There were little yellow flowers everywhere, with their dark yellow center. Then there were very small flowers shaped like daisies, but they were lavender; and also huge flowers that resembled Texas bluebonnets, reminding me of the days as a young boy when my parents took us to the countryside in April to play and roll in the bluebonnets. And then there were the mosses of every shade of green – some that I would call "neon" green – spectacular in their own right. Finally there were tiny white "cluster daisies," I called them – very small, growing in clusters of fifteen or twenty, each with their tiny yellow center. All of these were framed by gorgeous ferns that were very fine, like lace, and by various species of grass – elegant shapes in many shades of green.

I spent my days sitting alongside the stream, among all of these flowers and plants, looking southeast at the Wind River Range, which was over two hundred miles away in Wyoming. To my back, about fifteen or twenty meters away, was an area of all rocks – it was a rockslide rising sharply to the northwest formed of rocks that had fallen over the decades from the butte lying to the north.

About a half hour before dusk, all of a sudden I sat up with the impulse to walk behind me to the rockslide. I went with my instinct, but in the midst of doing so, I remember wondering, "Why am I doing this? The sound of the stream and the wildflowers are my perfect place. Why am I leaving it to go there?" But as I walked up the slide of rocks, I noticed a very large flat rock just in front of me – perhaps ten meters away. I saw something move on top of it and I stopped dead in my tracks. Was it a person? I couldn't make it out; so I reached in my shirt pocket and put on my glasses, just as it was getting up. It was a mountain lion!

Standing frozen, I watched as she stood up on the rock, silhouetting herself against the sky. She stood motionless for a while, looking directly at me. Then she turned around on top of the rock, pirouetting as if to show me how beautiful and powerful she was. She did this twice, turning around fully as I locked in on her, transfixed. When she finished, she looked again directly at me fixing her gaze on my eyes. Then suddenly she turned west, and with a gigantic leap off the rock, she disappeared.

Immediately as she left, I used my two-way radio to contact the guides at the three solo sites about a half-mile west of me, directly in the path she was running. They never saw her.

I collected myself, sitting down, right there on the rocks where I had been standing. I stayed there for the longest time, stunned at the power of the mountain lion's presence and by her beauty. The strongest image of her that remains is when she leapt off the rock. I learned later that the mountain lion can leap over forty feet, and I'm certain it was that far. It was an arc silhouetted against the sky, effortless and full of grace. And I'll never forget her tail – it seemed almost as long as her body and carried a presence of its own.

I made my way down to the stream and the flowers, reflecting on my experience. Within just ten minutes, the thought came to me: "I know what to do." I pulled out my little note pad from my shirt pocket and wrote: ""I will focus on a more evolved, more powerful model of the U-process. That is what I will devote the coming years to."

When we returned to the high base camp the following day, I spoke to Tini and Wanda, the two guides who had first taken us to Black Butte on horseback four years earlier. Wanda, a Native American, was clear about this encounter: "We consider a meeting like that as a totem. We can live in these mountains a lifetime and never see a mountain lion – it's a blessing to have met her. There's an important lesson here; use it wisely." Brian, who was part of our team, underscored what Wanda said and suggested some books that could help me.

I learned that the early Native American stories and myths speak of a magical time in which there were no boundaries between humans and animals. Always, the divine revealed itself in nature, through the ancient knowledge of spirit animals. The animals become our friends, our teachers, and our companions, and they speak to us through their appearances, behaviors, movements, and characteristic patterns. When we know what to look for, we can use them, as Wanda said, as totems for high knowledge and higher perception. They touch a primal part of our heart and soul – and stir long-dormant embers.

I learned that the mountain lion is one of the largest cats in the Western Hemisphere. It is one of the fastest and most powerful of all animals. The Native Americans said if the mountain lion shows up in your life, it's time to focus on power. When she shows up as a totem, much of the trial has been worked through – now is the time to assert and be prepared to grow past the status quo. When the mountain lion shows up, there is a choice to be made. This choice should be made quickly and strongly, but asserted gently. The mountain lion teaches self-efficacy – to take charge of one's life circumstances effectively, and to do so in a mindful way.

9. LEARNING HARD LESSONS

HOW DO WE FILL THE WORLD WITH CONTEMPORARY SAGES AND KICK-ASS SAINTS,
WHO ARE AS ADEPT AT SURRENDERING THEMSELVES TO THE SILENCE AS THEY ARE
AT INNOVATING INITIATIVES OF BREATHTAKING POWER?
– Robert Rabbin

After my encounter with the mountain lion, I began an intense period of reflection, looking back at all that had occurred since that moment of commitment in Baja, especially my founding of GLI and the demonstration projects. I came away with two core lessons. First, I learned about the power of sudden illumination: when strong intimations arise, as they did on that high bluff in Baja, go with them. Don't get caught up in thinking about them, but be open and allow yourself to be used "as a force of nature," as George Bernard Shaw put it. Second, and most important, I learned that the conscious development of facilitators is paramount.

My sensitivity to this crucial element was raised by reading a memorandum sent to Zaid Hassan, a colleague of mine in Generon with whom I closely worked during the years of the demonstration projects. It came from Robert Rabbin, an acquaintance of Zaid and a recognized authority on personal development and self-awareness:

> I know that you have addressed the issue of constant "presencing" even after that phase of the process is over, and I love this attention to Silence you have given in the Global Leadership Change Lab. I wonder if you have accounted for something that could happen: though Senge, et al., have not pointed this out, there is (in my experiences and to use their U model) a little doorway at the bottom of the U that is like a rabbit hole to non-being. If one slips through that doorway

and is taken by non-being, one cannot be certain that the upward curve of the U will still be valid when being kicks in. When people fall into the rabbit hole of non-being, the nature of their being is changed. The nature of their will is changed. The nature of their speaking is changed. We come to words like "surrender" and "devotion." We come to the intersection of time and timelessness, of effort and grace, of doing and non-doing – of living beyond defining dualities and the seeming invincibility of our ideas. . . . Will this be spoken about in your Lab, and will it be demonstrated? *Will your facilitators have the qualities and character to embody and transmit this great true and simple thing that since the beginning of time has set fire to souls and aroused their infinite capacities to build arks, and not for animals, but for love?* [Emphasis added.]

I'm thinking of a story that is supposed to be true: . . . During the partition the violence in Calcutta was terrible, and Gandhi was broken hearted. He went to the city, took up residence on the verandah of a large house, and sent out the word that he was going to fast until death, or until all of the violence had stopped. Day after day, his aid[e]s reported a lessening of violence, urging him to eat. He wouldn't. He was already old and frail, but he did not waver. The word spread of his vow. Slowly, the violence dissipated. After a few days, only sporadic attacks. His aid[e]s begged him to eat. No. Not until ALL the violence stopped. Finally, it did. Everyone laid down their hatred, their fear, their weapons. The violence stopped. It was as if Gandhi's incredible spiritual force lifted everyone else up to an equivalent place.

Will the Global Leadership Change Lab make these kinds of "legendary" leaders who, by their very presence, will call people and cause people to rise up to their higher selves in real and telling ways? I wonder if the "missing" element in your draft is around the qualities and character of your facilitators. Perhaps a component of the curriculum could include studying Rumi, Hafiz and others? Case studies such as the one above? Perhaps my caution is to use the models and process, but not to be used by them. How do we fill the world with contemporary sages and kick-ass saints, who are as adept at surrendering themselves to the Silence as they are at innovating initiatives of breathtaking power? How do emerging leaders keep pace with being and non-being at the same time? I have an idea that emerging leaders should be the very embodiment of such a process, much the same way as Gandhi on the verandah.

– Robert Rabbin

Rabbin raised the central question that defined how I would focus my life energy in the years to come: the development of people who are of sufficient maturity to enable connection to Brian's "deeper place of knowing."

One of Generon's founding partners, Bill O'Brien, often told me that "the success of an intervention is dependent on the inner state of the intervener." By this time, a number of books and articles and many workshops worldwide had grown out of experiments with the U-process, and there was a continuing interest in the process and the U-theory as well as in what enables the U-process to produce remarkable results. But I became convinced that we were paying insufficient attention to O'Brien's injunction.

During this entire time, from 2000 through 2007, I remained vaguely unsettled. For me, the explanations of the U-theory in hundreds of pages of books and articles were missing something vital, particularly when they attempted to describe what happens at the "bottom" of the U. At times, we came close to an adequate explanation – but then we fell back into overanalytic ways of describing what occurs there. As my colleagues and I wrote about "redirection" in *Presence*, a book published during that time, I kept thinking, "Something this fundamental is deeply important. We need to understand how people can access and utilize this force at the bottom of the U."

The pattern of success in the three demonstration projects served to reinforce this conviction. We commissioned a "learning history" for each project. These learning histories reflected the remarkable results each project had produced; but it was clear that the Food Lab and Meadowlark had achieved a greater level of initial success than the PCN. Both the Food Lab and the PCN had a "moonshot" quality about them in terms of their sheer size and complexity. But while the Food Lab had met our highest expectations, the PCN had not. The learning histories and our own assessment were clear: we had put greater time and attention into the development of the facilitators and workshop leaders in the Food Lab than had been possible in the PCN.

A lead funder of the Food Lab project was the W.K. Kellogg Foundation of Battle Creek, Michigan, one of the world's largest private foundations. The night before we made our presentation for funding to the senior officers of the foundation, we were invited for dinner at the home of the head of agricultural programs at Kellogg, Oran Hesterman, and his wife Linda. The senior vice president, a board member who was principally responsible for approving the largest grants, was also present that evening.

As we began dinner, Oran asked about the distinguishing features of our approach to the Food Lab – what made the Lab such a powerful tool for collective innovation and problem solving. For some reason, instead of giving the standard low-key response, I began telling Oran about our meeting with Brian and the work he did in Hong Kong with his Taoist teacher to prepare himself for gaining access to "that deeper place of knowing." Rather than the look of puzzlement I almost expected, both Oran and Linda expressed complete understanding of what Brian was describing and what we had designed into the Lab.

As it turned out, both Oran and Linda had been studying this domain for years – how one or many can gain access to sudden illumination by choosing to follow a disciplined path toward self-realization through contemplative practices: meditation, yoga, qigong, and direct exposure to the generative processes of nature.

A profoundly deep dialogue about these matters took place over several hours at Oran's home that night. The presentations the next morning, as it turned out, were a mere formality. The decision had been made that night over dinner. Kellogg effectively joined Unilever as a lead funder for the entire undertaking. Oran joined as an active champion for enrolling other key funders and sponsors, ensuring the success of the organizational phase of the SFL.

One of the early sessions of the Food Lab was a multiday Innovation Retreat similar to the one we used during the Alliance project to correspond to Brian's "retreat and reflect – go to that deeper place of knowing." Those participating were representatives of the thirty or so founding participants – the multisector group representing a microcosm of the whole system in question. We had "the system in the room," so to speak.

The retreat took place in the foothills of the Santa Rita Mountains of Arizona and was co-led by Susan, whose responsibilities included serving as Generon's Director of Retreats. Brian and other members of the Generon team were also there. Susan had trained with John Milton over the previous three years. John had told me that during the first day of her awareness training, he had the intuition to give her the *advanced* awareness training. Susan, through years of individual practice and personal discipline, had refined her capacity for other ways of knowing that superseded the ordinary. So with Susan and Brian deeply involved with the design and delivery of the early elements of the Lab, including the retreat, the core Lab team had the foundational training required for the superior success of the project. The experience of the team on the retreat set the tone for the entire Lab.

During the retreat, the team had a two-night solo experience in the wilderness where the solo tents of the team members were separated by about a half mile. At the conclusion of the solo, the team gathered in a circle to share their experience, just as we have designed all of our Lab retreats. As the team went around the circle, reporting one by one, it occurred that two of the participants had *precisely* the same dream on the solo. That was just one indicator of the deep interconnectedness the team shared, enabling them to powerfully focus on solving the problem at hand as "a single intelligence."

Of that experience, Oran reported later to the learning historian: "I have never seen a process quite like this for bringing a very diverse group to a profound place of connection with one another and with what it is we are here to do."

10. ENCOUNTER IN THE
NETHERLANDS

*THE ROLE OF THE FACILITATOR — AND THE STATE OF THE
FACILITATOR'S CONSCIOUSNESS — IS CRITICALLY IMPORTANT TO
ENABLING CREATIVE DISCOVERY WHILE USING THE U-PROCESS.*

In November 2007, I had a highly illuminating encounter with a participant in a master class I was delivering in the Netherlands, an encounter that ultimately helped confirm my core learning from all that had occurred since the salon and helped inform my work going forward.

I was delivering the workshop with Betty Sue Flowers at Nijenrode University near Amsterdam. When we finished, a number of the participants came up to talk with us, and I fell into a conversation about Baja with someone when suddenly a young woman interrupted us, with apologies, and said, "Have you heard of Bernard Lievegoed and the U-methodology he uses?"

Astonished, I said "No – but I can sense the connection." At this point, Betty Sue told me that the taxi was waiting to take us to the airport, so I quickly wrote down the woman's name, Annemieke Korte, and her email address.

For the next year, we emailed back and forth. Annemieke told me that she was in the process of writing a manuscript for a book to be published about the kind of organization that is required to create a truly healing climate for children with severe trauma, developmental disorders, or mental handicaps. She had read *Synchronicity* and *Presence* and had been drawn to the workshop to find inspiration for completing her book. She worked at Zonnehuizen, a highly regarded academy for children with the disabilities she had described, founded by Bernard Lievegoed, a distinguished physician, author, educator, and industrial psychologist.

Lievegoed had been director of Zonnehuizen from its founding until 1954, when he founded the Nederlands Pedagogisch Instituut (the Netherlands Pedagogical Institute, or NPI), which was an institute for organizational development. He led NPI for the next seventeen years, and it became his life's work.

I discovered that the main feature the NPI "U-procedure" had in common with the U-theory we had developed using Brian Arthur's insights was the figure of the U itself. The moment Otto drew the first U in the parking lot at Xerox PARC, I found the downward movement perfectly representative of the courage, the act of will it takes to reach for that "place of deeper knowing" and to act on it. We used the figure U to "envision and model one single process with seven distinct aspects or practices."

One reason I hadn't heard of the European version of the U-procedure was that it was better known in Europe as the "NPI Method" – which is why Annemieke thought Lievegoed had created it. In fact, Friedrich Glasl and Dirk Lemson developed the U-methodology, first presenting it in an internal NPI paper in 1969.

While learning that there was a European "U" was interesting, the deeper gift to me in the encounter with Annemieke was coming to know the other work of Glasl and of Lievegoed himself, who published more than thirty best-selling books, his last finished ten days before his death in 1992. Many of his books deeply inform the inner journey humans take toward releasing their full capacity.

In *Man on the Threshold*, Lievegoed describes how humanity is experiencing a fundamental change in consciousness. The perceived boundaries that surrounded consciousness for centuries are no longer fixed, and as we shall see, it is no longer only the physical world that implies reality. *Phases – The Spiritual Rhythm of Adult Life* charts the milestones humans pass through from adolescence through old age, milestones that are universal in nature. Regardless of background, everyone must pass through critical outer and inner stages, like those of the hero's journey that the mythographer Joseph Campbell had described.

In *The Developing Organization*, Glasl and Lievegoed describe four phases of organizational development (the pioneer; the differentiated; the integrated; and the associative phases) and compare them to the evolution of human consciousness. Later, Glasl published *The Enterprise of the Future: Moral Intuition in Leadership and the Organization's Development*. (In both these books, the authors refer to the "U-procedure" as a methodology of self-diagnosis, self-discovery, and planning.)

My conversations and correspondence with Annemieke confirmed my growing conviction that the role of the facilitator – and *the state of the facilitator's consciousness* – is critically important to enabling creative discovery while using the U-process. During the Demonstration Projects, I had often seen the walls of separateness among the group dissolve and had seen the group tap into levels of creativity beyond their separate capacity.

An early example of this phenomenon was during the Food Lab Innovation Retreat. I had also seen projects and processes where the walls failed to dissolve. I determined to look more deeply into the "mystery" that occurs at the bottom of the U in order to develop a more precise theoretical understanding about what Rabbin had described as the "little doorway at the bottom of the U that is like a rabbit hole to non-being" and "set[s] fire to souls," enabling leaders to tap their infinite capacity to "build arks, not for animals, but for love."

11. STAGE IV LEADERS

SERVANT LEADERSHIP ALONE IS NO LONGER ADEQUATE
TO THE HIGH CHALLENGES PREVAILING TODAY.

Soon after my conversation with Annemieke in the Netherlands, I was in New York City for several days of meetings with Tex. When our business meetings had concluded, Tex invited me to spend a half day with him and an acquaintance who was a specialist in human development and organizational transformation. Our conversation focused on developmental models like the ones Lievegoed and Glasl had written about beginning in the 1960s in which they had presented the four phases of the developing organization and compared them to the evolution of human consciousness. Tex spoke that day of an acquaintance, M. Scott Peck, who wrote the international best seller, *The Road Less Traveled.* Tex's comments that day led me to reread Peck's books.

In the late 1980s, Peck published *The Different Drum: Community Making and Peace.* During the dozen years while Peck was working on the book, he served as a mentor to Kaz, introducing him to a model of communal growth that Kaz later introduced to me. Like Lievegold and Glasl, Peck identified four progressive stages in human development that both individuals and organizations pass through and that are found across cultures and geographic boundaries.

A week after meeting Tex, I began to study Kaz's dissertation along with an essay Kaz had published with Robert Frager, one of the founders of Transpersonal Psychology. That essay described a version of Peck's four stages of human development in terms of organizational leaders, using insights Kaz and I had gained working together on a complex organizational transformation in the 1990s.

Using these ideas and experiences, along with my earlier work with the American Leadership Forum, Kaz and I developed Peck's stages of spiritual development into four stages of organizational leadership development. Of course there are many gradations between stages, and even the most developed of us often move back and forth between levels, particularly in the later stages.

Stage I: Self-centric Leaders – Characteristic of young people and perhaps 20 percent of adults, this is a stage of undeveloped spirituality. Members of this group are generally incapable of loving others. They may appear to be loving (and think of themselves that way), but their relationships with their fellow human beings are all essentially manipulative and self-serving. They are unprincipled, governed by little but their own will. And since the will may shift from moment to moment, there is a lack of integrity in their being. Some may be quite disciplined in the service of expediency and their own ambition and so may rise to positions of considerable prestige and power. Some, occasionally, advance to Stage II.

Stage II: Achieving Leaders – These are people who mature to the point of valuing others. Their self-identity may include family, peers, organizations, faith groups, or nations. Stability is a principal value for people in this stage. They seek to conform to the established rules of their faith or organization and may feel disconcerted or threatened if someone seems to be playing the game outside these rules. Their pursuit of excellence is characterized by fairness, decency, and respect for others. They routinely succeed in their organizational goals because they genuinely value others. Their achievements are a reflection of their self-discipline. As they rise in organizational power and influence in the later phases of their Stage II development, they develop and strengthen others as well. In these later phases, their achievements are accomplished with and through others.

Stage III: Servant Leaders – This stage of development is marked by an even greater expansion of self to embrace all people, regardless of race, gender, class, or creed. Stage III leaders routinely use their power and influence to serve and develop others. In Robert Greenleaf's terms, those around them become healthier, wiser, more autonomous, and more independent – and more likely to become servant leaders. These leaders are routinely entrusted with leading teams with important institutional assets and with entire organizations. This is a stage of growth that questions rigid belief systems and transcends conventional rules and roles.

People at this stage of development exhibit a high need for achievement, yet not at the cost of others in their organization or in society at large. They have a high need for independence and a low need for conformity. They have a high propensity for mature risk taking, a strong sense of self-efficacy, and a tolerance of ambiguity. Accordingly, they thrive in times of turbulence and complexity. They have adopted a systems view of the world. In the more advanced phase of this stage, they gain stronger awareness of the interconnectedness of all life. In their organizations, they nurture understanding of and responsibility for the larger social systems within which the individual and organization operate.

Servant Leadership alone is no longer adequate to the high challenges prevailing today. Our institutions must be led by a more advanced generation of "Renewing Leaders" or "Stage IV" leaders.

Stage IV: Renewing Leaders – Stage IV leaders embody the characteristics and values of servant leaders but have matured to a more comprehensive and subtle level of development. They exhibit a capacity for extraordinary functioning and performance. At the heart of this kind of performance is a capacity for tacit knowing that can be used for breakthrough thinking, strategy formation, operational excellence, and innovation, including envisioning and creating the kind of organization or society we desire.

Stage IV leaders hold the conviction that there is an underlying intelligence within the universe that is capable of guiding us and preparing us for the futures we must create. They combine their cognitive understanding of the world around them with a strong interior knowledge of the hidden potentials lying dormant in the universe – a view that carries with it the power to change the world as we know it.

12. RETURN TO BAJA

MOST GREAT INVENTIONS AND BREAKTHROUGHS HAVE ARISEN
THROUGH DEEP COMMUNION WITH SOURCE.
– John Milton

I had been in touch with John Milton regularly over the years since my first trip to Baja and the birth of the Global Leadership Initiative. In a telephone call one morning, I told John about my intense interest in learning more about how people develop sufficient mastery to connect to Brian's "place of deeper knowing."

"If I ever write another book," I told John, "it's going to be about the extraordinary functioning of human beings, individual and collectively – and specifically how developmentally advanced leaders can learn to reliably sense and actualize new realities. This ability to actualize hidden potential lying dormant in the universe carries with it the power to change the world as we know it."

John suggested I return to Baja for another wilderness passage to gain insight and inspiration for the next phase of my life and for the explorations I was undertaking.

At the conclusion of the first four days of awareness training, John began instructing us to select our solo sites. He drew a little map of the coastline, as he usually does. When he got to a remote point on his map, he said, "Now this site is one for the truly adventurous"

On impulse, I said, "OK, I'll take that site."

The next day, on the way to the trailhead, I began wondering if I had been too hasty in my selection. John simply said, "You'll be fine." I still had my doubts, but it was too late to turn back.

Late in the afternoon, as I made my way down to the site, I saw what John was warning us about. I had to climb over an immense line of boulders jutting far out into the sea. The only way across was next to a place where the waves were thundering up onto the boulders. I had a sixty-pound pack on my back and had to time my crossing to avoid being pounded by the surf and pulled out to sea. I had to cross this line three times going in and once going out – one time in with my pack, another time returning for my jerry can of water at the trailhead, and the third to my camp site with the water. Each trip, from one end to the other, was about six miles.

The solo itself was serene, deep but uneventful. I was a little disappointed that I did not have another breakthrough experience as I had had with the two whales. But at the conclusion of the awareness training, John had made the point that every passage in the wilderness carries its own rhythm. The experience is more like a time-release capsule in that the lessons tend to unfold over time – weeks, months, and even years.

On the final day of the awareness training, John spoke briefly to the explorations I was undertaking. He said, "The Great Mystery is the underlying reality out of which all forms, including you yourself, manifest. It is primordial and formless, yet gives birth to all forms, holds all forms. It is infinite and beyond all conventional measurements and descriptions. This is why I call it 'the Great Mystery.'"

He continued, "The Taoists refer to it as 'Source.' The closer one approaches Source, the more synchronous events become. When Source is accessed, extraordinary creativity occurs. Most great inventions and breakthroughs have arisen through deep communion with Source."

John said that he always reserves his further teaching about Source for his advanced awareness training and invited us to begin working toward that end. As he paused for a moment, I asked, "John, what's the difference between God and Source?"

John reflected for just a moment. Then, with an almost imperceptible smile, replied, "Joseph, there's a thin line between the two. At a later time, we can talk about it." He then turned to the group to continue his teaching.

I returned home the next day, committing to exploring the latest research on knowledge creation and the relationship of the teaching of Tibetan Buddhist and Taoist masters on the subject.

Two weeks later, I received an invitation confirming a meeting that furnished the perfect vehicle for that exploration.

13. JOURNEY TO PARI

THE REALITY WHICH IS MOST IMMEDIATE TO US CANNOT BE STATED.
– David Bohm

The letter was from F. David Peat, a noted physicist and author with whom I had corresponded over the years. David was a friend and colleague of David Bohm for more than twenty years. Together they wrote *Science, Order and Creativity*. David was writing to invite me to a conference on "The Legacy of David Bohm" to be held at the Pari Center in the medieval hilltop village of Pari, Italy, south of Siena, in June of 2008. The meeting would take place as a roundtable of about fifteen people to encourage open discussion, he said, and would begin with a short technical session for the physicists and mathematicians. It would then open out to a discussion of the implications of Bohm's work for society as a whole. The list of attendees included many of Bohm's long-time collaborators and early students, many of whom had written papers and books on Bohm's approach to physics.

I couldn't accept quickly enough. I had first met Bohm on a Monday morning in the summer of 1980. The Friday before, I had left the law firm I had helped establish twenty years earlier in order to follow a dream I had held for over six years – to found a new leadership forum in America. The American Leadership Forum was designed to introduce a developmental path to rising leaders who were committed to becoming servant leaders. After reading a lead article in the *Sunday Times* about his new book, *Wholeness and the Implicate Order*, I followed my immediate impulse and went to the telephone. After several calls, I found Bohm's home number, and before I knew it, he was at the other end of the line.

I poured my heart out to him, telling him what I was all about and that I must see him. Almost without hesitation, he agreed to spend the next afternoon with me. I spent over four hours with him, tape-recording our conversation. What he told me provided the foundational elements of the curriculum for the Forum and turned out to be one of the most important days of my life. What I learned that day altered my worldview forever, creating the opening for all that occurred afterward.

After our meeting, I moved to Houston to found the Forum. A couple of months later, I received a handwritten letter from Bohm saying how much he had enjoyed our conversation and how much he hoped we could meet again soon to continue the dialogue. I responded the following day, but allowed the press of founding and running the Forum to get in the way of returning to meet with him. I called him after arriving back in London, but by that time he was too ill to meet with me and passed away a year later.

I count this as one of the greatest mistakes of my life – I've regretted it ever since. I acknowledged it in *Synchronicity* – and wrote about the "Trap of Over-activity" as one of the patterns in my life that blocked my full development. I solemnly swore to myself that I would never, ever do that again – that I would do my best to "de-clutter" my life, making room for opportunities and blessings that show up at the most "inopportune" times.

When I read the invitation from David Peat, I saw this as a sort of reprieve – an opportunity to correct, in some measure, the terrible mistake I had made earlier. That day, when I accepted David's invitation, I had that feeling of excitement and anticipation that accompanies breakthrough moments – and in fact, came away from the meeting in Pari with two key gifts. The first was a much deeper insight into what Bohm had told me about the nature of the universe; and the second was an introduction to one of the world's most respected living scientists, the – dean emeritus of Princeton's School of Engineering.

Both led me to formulate principles that helped complete my understanding of what I had been struggling to comprehend for so many years. By the time I had left Baja for the second time, I had developed the concept of the source of discovery, creation, renewal, and transformation, but I had not yet been able to explain that concept. Without that step, my understanding was incomplete.

I left for Pari a week early to go to a hotel in the little village of
Colle Val d'Elsa, lying between Florence and Pari, in order to review all
I had read about Bohm since I had first met him. In rereading all the
books, papers, and essays, I was reminded of how respected Bohm was
among his peers. He was acknowledged as a brilliant physicist, explorer of
consciousness, and one of the most original thinkers of the second half of
the twentieth century, a man who had made influential contributions to
physics, philosophy, consciousness, psychology, language, and education.
Einstein had such a high regard for Bohm and his work that he made
Bohm his close collaborator and friend.

Bohm came to believe that the traditional interpretation of quantum
mechanics, with its issues associated with uncertainty, was incomplete.
In a bold step that turned quantum mechanics on its head, he introduced
the "implicate order," which created a storm of controversy, yet may well
have opened the door to a much deeper theory of the nature of reality and
existence.

The day before the conference, I drove south from Colle Val d'Elsa
to Pari. A map of the year 1250 shows the village much as it is today,
surrounded by a heavily wooded area and, closer to the village itself, by
olive groves and vineyards. I learned later that the woods are filled with
wild boar, deer, and pheasants, and that the families of Pari grow their
fruits and vegetables according to traditional farming methods on the
surrounding land. Only two hundred people live in the little medieval
village, which has a small hotel, a grocer, a general store, a post office, a
hairdresser, and one restaurant, which serves traditional Tuscan cooking.

I checked into the small hotel and walked up to the meeting room at
the top of the village. The original building at the summit had once been
a castle. The views from there were magnificent. I could see the forest,
olive groves, and vineyards for miles. And it was serene – so quiet. I could
sense the energy field there as I walked into the empty meeting room. It
was set up with a long conference table, flip charts, and a huge blackboard
on a stand. Windows on two sides filled the room with light, and out one
of them, I saw a little park.

I had learned that David Peat had created the Pari Center for New Learning with his wife, Maureen Doolan, and the support of the village associates, Sette Colli (Seven Hills), and the Comune di Civitella Paganico. The Center is dedicated to education, learning, and research and encourages an interdisciplinary approach linking science, the arts, ethics, and spirituality. Its philosophy and approach is that of "gentle action." Above all, David Peat had told me, the Center is dedicated to the "spirit of place" – what Ikujiro Nonaka called "*ba.*" As I made my way down the steep steps to the village center, where we were to have dinner, I felt deep gratitude for the opportunity to meet with Bohm's colleagues and students in such simple, serene, and beautiful surroundings.

Dinner was planned for seven o'clock at the village association's meeting room – a long, narrow room with a table that ran the entire length of the room. As I approached the door, I could see that the meal was already being served by Maureen and Eleanor (David and Maureen's daughter) with the help of others, some of whom appeared to be local women.

Just outside the door, I met a young man who introduced himself as Tahir Gozel. I recognized his name because he was listed on the invitation as the person who had supported the entire affair, including all of our travel, food, and accommodation expenses. Tahir was a highly successful businessman and philanthropist from Baku, Azerbaijan, a member of the Society for Organizational Learning (SoL), and, as he told me later, a long-time student of Bohm's, having first learned of him by reading my *Synchronicity* book years before. Tahir was accompanied by two young friends from Turkey who were members of SoL Turkey and who had agreed to prepare a report of the proceedings.

Tahir introduced me to David, Maureen, and Eleanor, and David, in turn, introduced me to all the others. It was a bit overwhelming at first because I was meeting so many people at once whom I had read about and for whom I held deep admiration and respect. The sheer number was a lot to take in – it reminded me a little of the way I had felt on the first day as a fraternity "pledge" at the University of Texas, meeting all the members at once.

There was Basil Hiley, Bohm's long-time collaborator. I knew Hiley's name instantly because it had been mentioned throughout all the books

I had read about Bohm. As I learned during the course of the meeting, Hiley had been utterly devoted to Bohm and all Bohm stood for, having been his student at Birkbeck in the 1960s. I learned from many of those present that Bohm was equally devoted to Basil. For the next few days, I stuck pretty close to Basil and David, who were both tolerant of my incessant questions and had the capacity to translate complicated conversations among the physicists into clear and concise accounts for me.

I met Yakir Aharanov, a pioneer in quantum theory and a distinguished Israeli professor of physics at Chapman University, who was an early student of Bohm. Aharanov and Bohm discovered what came to be known as the Aharanov-Bohm Effect, or AB Effect, making explicit the essential, global nature of quantum theory. The work of Aharanov and Bohm was considered by many physicists to be of Nobel Prize quality, and over the years, rumors circulated that they were short-listed for the prize but never won it because of ambiguity over who exactly had discovered the effect.

That night I also met Henri Bortoft, a former student of Bohm and an apprentice to Bohm in the 1960s, who has focused much of his life's work on Goethe's approach to science. I had known of his comprehensive book on the philosophy of Goethe's science, so I was delighted to meet him. Otto had interviewed Bortoft as part of our research leading to the U-process. In fact, we had used Bortoft's insights on observing, suspending, and redirecting our attention in the opening pages of our book *Presence.* Bortoft called the focus on an understanding of the generative process underlying reality, "encountering the authentic whole."

Then there was Lee Nichol, who had worked with Bohm closely on the phenomenon of dialogue and the potential of the collective intelligence inherent in highly aligned groups to beneficially affect the trajectory of an organization – or, if the dialogue involves sufficient numbers, the trajectory of our current civilization. That, of course, was at the very heart of Bohm's injunction to me in London, so it was natural that I spent a good bit of time with Lee at meals and in between sessions.

I also met Mark Edwards of London, one of the most widely published editorial photographers in the world and founder of a photo agency specializing in environmental issues, the third world, and nature. He is the coauthor, with Bohm, of *Changing Consciousness*, which focuses on thought and its manifestation in terms of society and the planet.

In addition to the many remarkable physicists and mathematicians present, I also discovered that an old friend of mine was present, Andrew Stone, Lord Stone of Blackheath, a member of the House of Lords in the United Kingdom and former chief executive officer of Marks & Spencer, who was in the process of establishing a department of Religion and Science at the University of Cairo. I had met Andrew years earlier in London and knew of his reputation as a servant leader in his organization. True to his character, as I sat down next to Tahir for dinner, it was Andrew who arrived from the kitchen with my dinner plate, placing it in front of me and asking if there was anything else I needed.

14. THE FINITE, THE INFINITE, AND THE DESTINY STATE

THIS ENERGY, OR SPIRIT, INFUSES ALL LIVING BEINGS, AND WITHOUT IT ANY ORGANISM MUST FALL APART INTO ITS CONSTITUENT ELEMENTS.
– David Bohm

The next morning, David convened the meeting by reading a short piece Bohm had written in 1987 to be read at the memorial service for a lifelong friend, a classmate of Bohm's at Penn State University. The piece was later read at Bohm's own memorial service at Birkbeck College:

> The field of the finite is all that we can see, hear, touch, remember, and describe. This field is basically that which is manifest, or tangible. The essential quality of the infinite, by contrast, is its subtlety, its intangibility. This quality is conveyed in the word *spirit*, whose root meaning is "wind or breath." This suggests an invisible but pervasive energy to which the manifest world of the finite responds. This energy, or spirit, infuses all living beings, and without it any organism must fall apart into its constituent elements. That which is truly alive in the living being is this energy of spirit, and this is never born and never dies.

After David concluded, he stood without comment while we all absorbed what had been read. The solemnity of the moment was manifest, the energy in the room palpable. Without further comment, David asked Basil Hiley, if he could, to be the first to present.

Basil spoke for about an hour, using the blackboard part of the time to write mathematical equations – very quickly, but in a fluid, sweeping way that I found completely absorbing. I had never seen a physicist "speak" this way before – it was a process and a language that would be repeated by the physicists that day and the next. At one point, Andrew and I exchanged glances, and he said, "The math – the beauty of it – we don't understand it at one level, but at another, we do completely. It's like listening to opera – in Italian."

At one point later in the day, Yakir was performing "opera" at the blackboard with his chalk. It was magnificent, although I couldn't understand any of it. But in the midst of it he exclaimed, "The Destiny State," paused a moment, and then went on writing at the blackboard. Later I found out from David that Yakir had been showing how to derive dynamic, living time out of the mathematics. He was showing that time, although it can run in reverse sequence, moves into the future, attracted by what he calls a *destiny state*. I found this to be a stunning statement – because it's exactly as I picture the dynamics of the universe and an unfolding future. It comports precisely with the guiding principles lying at the heart of the Stage IV organization and helps to explain why they are so successful: their unfolding future is driven by their strong sense of meaning and purpose.

Of all those in the room, Basil was the one who had worked most closely with Bohm for the longest period of time. He was Bohm's assistant. Bohm would have the original ideas. Basil would then work out the mathematics. Several days later, Basil would present his mathematics to Bohm, who appeared to have already arrived at the same point via intuition.

Throughout the later decades of his life, Bohm sought a *new order* in physics. According to Bohm, the ground, or essence, of the cosmos is not elementary particles, but pure process – a flowing movement of the whole. Within this new order, Bohm deeply believed one could resolve the ancient conception that mind and matter are separate – that mind cannot act on the material universe. It was his conviction that the entire universe is intricately connected – it is all about relationship – and that this is an undeniable, underlying truth. As Basil said that day to me, "Wholeness is built into the universe – there is no hierarchy.

Bohm's life was infused by a search for this truth, no matter what the consequences."

Basil and Bohm set out to search for this new order in physics, developing the idea of nonlocality in quantum theory, the implicate order, quantum potential, and the notion of active information.

15. NONLOCALITY AND THE
IMPLICATE ORDER

[THE IMPLICATE ORDER IS] NOT NECESSARILY A DESCRIPTION OF REALITY BUT A LANGUAGE, AN INNER LANGUAGE, WHERE YOU CANNOT ASSOCIATE EACH WORD TO A THING. IT'S MORE LIKE MUSIC
– David Bohm

At Bristol University in England, Bohm and Yakir demonstrated a new and important way in which the quantum world transcends the old physics of classical mechanics. They argued that even quite distant objects can affect quantum processes, an observation that is now known in physics as "nonlocality," or the Aharanov-Bohm Effect (AB Effect) – the work that the scientific journal *Nature* said was worthy of a Nobel Prize.

In the mid 1950s, one of Bohm's students encountered this prior work and was led in 1964 to propose what is now known as Bell's Theorem. It was confirmed experimentally eight years later by the physicist Alain Aspect at the University of Paris. In his 1975 US government–sponsored report, noted physicist Henry Stapp of the University of California at Berkeley said that Bell's Theorem is "the most profound discovery in the history of science." It proves, in effect, that the world is fundamentally inseparable.

The simplest explanation I can give of Bell's Theorem, based on what Bohm told me in London, is this: Imagine two paired particles in a two-particle system. If you make them fly apart or take them apart any distance – putting one particle in New York, say, and another in San Francisco – then if you change the spin of one of these particles, the other particle will *simultaneously* change its own spin. Bohm said "the effect is a simple consequence of the oneness of apparently separate objects." He said, "We are all one."

Bohm said the worldview of modern physics is now a systems view. Everything is connected to everything else. We are not entirely certain how this connectedness works, but we are certain that there is "separation without separateness." That is the way the universe is constructed – "the oneness implicate in Bell's Theorem envelops human beings and atoms alike."

This was a confirmation of the way I experienced reality, especially when I was backpacking in the wilderness. But to hear it from Bohm was radically disorienting – it shifted my worldview. We were talking about the essential interrelatedness and interdependence of all phenomena – physiological, social, and cultural. Nothing could be understood in isolation; everything had to be seen as a part of the unified whole.

⊱┈◈┈○┈◈┈⊰

In the late 1960s, Bohm introduced the idea of the *implicate order* as a way to describe the quantum universe. It was his attempt to create a new way of seeing and talking about the world: "It directs our attention away from boundaries and independent existences into holism, interconnectedness, and transformation."

The implicate order (from the Latin for "to be enfolded") is a level of reality beyond our normal, everyday thoughts and perceptions. All that we see around us is the world's surface, its explicate order. The implicate order lies far deeper. Out of the implicate, our explicate world unfolds.

In London, Bohm said to me that

> the implicate order is in the first instance a language. It's not necessarily a description of reality but a language, an inner language, where you cannot associate each word to a thing. It's more like music. You cannot say one note means anything. It's like a painting. There are various spots of paint in an impressionist painting, but when you step back to see the picture, there is no correspondence between the spots of paint and what you see in the picture. Similarly, the implicate order and its mathematics does not directly come to describe a sort of correspondence with reality. It is simply a language. This language is referring to something that cannot be stated. The reality which is most immediate to us cannot be stated.

David has pointed out that the implicate order is "both a philosophical attitude and a method of inquiry." And as Bohm sometimes used it, David says, the implicate order can "refer to a particular level of reality, a subtle material realm beyond the domain of particles and forces. In this sense, order is identified with essence."

The publication of *Wholeness and the Implicate Order* was announced on July 27, 1980, the Sunday before I met Bohm. I was immediately attracted to it, feeling that it explained the phenomenon of oneness I had experienced while playing sports on a highly aligned team and would provide the framework for the American Leadership Forum curriculum. I was not alone. Looking back, David wrote that the book and theory "had an immediate appeal . . . to writers, artists, musicians, psychologists and others who felt they had always experienced the world this way and now had access to a powerful common metaphor. . . . The important thing was the sense of liberation inherent in abandoning the old explicate order for the creative possibilities of the implicate order."

In a conversation late in the day, Basil and others agreed that, as opposed to just thinking about the implicate order abstractly, the most powerful way to acknowledge its existence is through *direct experience*. For example, when we are deeply absorbed in listening to beautiful music, we are directly experiencing the implicate. In the same way, the flow state we experience in running or in the midst of deep dialogue is the experience of the implicate. They agreed that the experience of flow exists in nature – we can't express it mathematically.

⋗⋅⋄⋅○⋅⋄⋅⋖

In conversations with David and others that first day, I learned that one of Bohm's guiding principles was that "nothing occurred in the universe that was without order." Peat noted that near the end of his life, Bohm "talked more and more about the need to discover order, rejecting anything that hinted at chance or randomness." This certainly coincided with everything I had experienced in my life, particularly after my commitment in London to form the Leadership Forum – from that point on, my life seemed to unfold according to a transcendent order. And this principle was at the heart of all I had learned during the process of uncovering the U.

Also, I learned that in the last years of his life, Bohm had spoken of the quantum potential in terms of a field of "active information." He proposed that information and its activity have an objective nature – that information occupies a central place in physics: "information must be placed alongside energy and matter as one of those factors underlying the processes of the universe." As David put it, "Bohm is now suggesting that information has an activity of its own. In particular, it in-forms or gives form to energy . . . thus, we must be open to the possibility that a new form of triad exists in the world." In other words, rather than simply matter and energy, we must think of matter, energy, and *information*.

At one level, this seems complicated and beyond the grasp of the nontechnical mind. But, to me, like the implicate order, Bohm's *field of active information* is entirely consistent with my direct experience and with all we learned during our research leading to the U-process. Bohm believed that the dialogue process was the active information that would clear up societal problems at the source. He argued that if the thinking process could be slowed down so that we could enter the "non-dual" state, we could "see from the inside." I take this to affirm precisely what we wrote in *The Red Book* and what Brian called "that place of deeper knowing."

>-+-4>-0-<+-+-<

The first evening concluded with Mark Edwards showing photographs he had taken all over the world. In July, 1969, Edwards was lost on the edge of the Sahara and was rescued by a Tuareg nomad, who took him to his people. The nomad made a fire and produced an old cassette player and played Bob Dylan singing "A Hard Rain's A-Gonna Fall." As Dylan piled image upon image, the idea came to Mark of illustrating each line of the song. In the years that followed, Mark traveled to over one hundred and fifty countries to fulfill his vision.

Mark's presentation that night was entitled "Hard Rain: Our Headlong Collision with Nature" – an unforgettable collection of his photographs illustrating Dylan's prophetic lyric. Mark spoke of the possibility of the "Sixth Great Extinction" that would occur because "we treat nature the way a master treats a slave." He concluded his presentation with this question: "Will we, our governments, the faith community, business leaders, media, and the arts be bold and brave enough to act? Or do we brace ourselves for a truly miserable descent into an environmental and social collapse?"

This question, I thought, was a fitting coda to the day and to Bohm's view of how our fragmented thought blocks civilization's creative advance.

16. INDIGENOUS SCIENCE

INDIGENOUS SCIENCE TEACHES THAT ALL THAT EXISTS
IS AN EXPRESSION OF RELATIONSHIPS — ALLIANCES AND BALANCES
BETWEEN ENERGIES, POWERS, AND SPIRITS.

The second day began with a conference call. The evening before, David had explained to those of us who didn't know him that Leroy Little Bear, a member of the Blackfoot tribe in Alberta, Canada, would join us for an hour or so by conference call. David explained that in the 1980s, he had begun exploring the more fundamental questions about quantum reality and the way our society had become separated and abstracted from nature. David was looking for a fresh approach that would help him explain his view that all nature, indeed the entire universe, is alive and vibrant.

David was in his study suffering writer's block — nothing would come to him. Suddenly a book caught his attention — *Touch the Earth*, which contained nineteenth-century photographs of Native American elders and leaders and included some of their speeches. As David began to read the first speech, the telephone rang. The person on the line announced himself as Leroy Little Bear. For over twenty years, David had unconsciously sought contact with a subtle and ancient culture, and now it was reaching him by telephone. For an instant, it felt to David as if one of the images from the book had sprung to life and was actually speaking to him.

Leroy was calling that day to invite David to a conference in Alberta where native elders and indigenous scientists would meet Western scientists to explore their different visions of reality. Leroy was a

philosopher within his Blackfoot traditions, but was also well acquainted
with Bohm's writings and the emerging view of quantum reality.

At that meeting were Iroquois, Blackfoot, Cree, Haida, Navaho, Hopi,
and Creek people, two aboriginal women from Australia, and several
Western scientists. That was David's introduction to the "indigenous
approach to knowing and being." This encounter led David to write
Blackfoot Physics, a book that was riveting for me to read in light of my
conversation with Bohm in London.

David's book is an account of his discoveries in the years since that
first conference in Alberta. He compares the myths, the languages, and
the perception of reality of the Western and the indigenous peoples.
What David reveals is an astonishing resemblance between indigenous
teachings and the insights that are now emerging from modern science
– including our understanding of ourselves, of different ways of knowing,
and of the universe and our place in it. Here is my synthesis of just four of
David's many discoveries:

- Quantum theory stresses the wholeness of all phenomena and
  the interconnectedness of nature. Indigenous science also holds
  that there is no separation between individual and society, matter
  and spirit, or each one of us and the whole of nature, and that
  wholeness is inherent within all of life.

- Bohm spoke of the implicate order, or enfolded order – an order
  in which the whole is enfolded in each part – as being a deeper
  physical reality than the surface, or explicate order, which is
  immediately perceived by our senses. In a similar way, members of
  the Gourd Society wear a necklace of mescal beads in which each
  bead symbolizes the cosmos and reminds them that each object is
  enfolded within the whole; indeed for those who wear it, it does
  enfold the universe and bring them in direct contact with all of
  creation.

- In modern physics, as Basil pointed out at Pari, the essential stuff
  of the universe cannot be reduced to billiard-ball atoms, but exists
  as relationships. Indigenous science teaches that all that exists is
  an expression of relationships – alliances and balances between
  energies, powers, and spirits.

- The leading-edge thinkers in physics – including all who were assembled in Pari – suggest that nature is not a collection of objects in interaction but is a flux of processes. The whole notion of flux and process is fundamental to the indigenous sciences.

After having read David's book, I was really looking forward to our call with Leroy. Lee Nichol, who also knew Leroy very well, took care of making the connection on the speakerphone. David and Lee greeted Leroy, introduced him to the group, and asked us to go around the table introducing ourselves by first and last name and telling where we lived. When we had done this, completing the circle, there was a brief pause. Then Leroy simply said: "I *see* you all there. Good to see you." There was a knowing silence in the room. I thought to myself, "He's not kidding! He really sees us."

We had a wide-ranging conversation about language ("I can talk Blackfoot all day long and not use a noun – only verbs. For us, everything is process and action-oriented"); time ("Beyond two days, everything else just is"); and the indigenous mind ("Our mind tolerates paradox and ambiguity because this order is closer to our inner structure of reality than a more mathematical form of logic").

A number of us had questions, which Leroy answered directly and concisely. Toward the end of our hour together, I told Leroy how powerful the wilderness retreats and solos I had participated in over the years had been. He mentioned that many nonnative people are drawn to the power of nature as a way of changing consciousness and that people all over the world have developed techniques for shifting consciousness. What really matters, he said, is not the state itself, but what the group and you do with it – how you act. In an indigenous context, the group has a great responsibility to the whole of society, especially to its harmony and balance.

With that, Leroy said his goodbyes.

>─┼─◆─●─◆─┼─◄

At the break that morning, Tahir and I took a short walk up to the top of the village. We sat on a bench in a little park just outside the window of our meeting room. He commented on Leroy's opening statement to us: "I see you all there. Good to see you." We knew that Leroy meant this literally; he had not lost the ancient capacity to naturally communicate over long distances. Tahir commented that this is entirely consistent with Bell's Theorem and an interconnected universe. Then I told him about a similar experience of a friend of mine, Lynne Twist, a veteran global activist and fundraiser, living in San Francisco with her husband Bill, a highly successful businessman and investor.

The story began in 1994 at a time when Lynne was responsible for managing fundraising operations in forty-seven countries for The Hunger Project. She was a founding executive of the Project in the 1970s and helped build it to a global movement to get at the root causes of world hunger – "why we would be living in a world awash with food, and yet 40,000 people a day are dying of hunger and starvation, most of them children under five." It wasn't a food problem, a distribution problem, or a human development problem, she and her colleagues determined – solving any of which would be a noble undertaking – but "it was a breakdown in the consciousness of the human family that we would allow so many of us – mostly children – to go hungry." It was, in Lynne's view, an issue of integrity. "We have gone numb to our relatedness to one another."

In 1994, Lynne and a colleague, John Perkins, a noted author who had worked for years in the Amazon rainforest with indigenous people there, traveled to Guatemala with a group of philanthropists who intended to work in the highlands of Guatemala with the Mayan people.

One night Lynne, John, and thirteen others from the group of donors met with a Mayan elder, a shaman, who was working with the Mayan people in that geographic area. They were sitting in a circle around a fire (one of the most ancient of social structures) at midnight, participating in a shamanic ceremony. John, who spoke Spanish and some Mayan, interpreted for the shaman, who instructed everyone to lie down with their feet facing the fire and close their eyes. The shaman began chanting and drumming, and Lynne fell into a kind of deep trance or dream state. In the dream, she became a huge bird flying over a vast unending forest of green. At a certain point, she, the bird, saw disembodied faces of men float up from the forest floor. They had orange geometric paint on their faces and yellow and red feather crowns on their heads. They called to her, the bird, in a strange language. Then they floated back down deep into the forest. A number of times they appeared and floated up to her and spoke – and then disappeared again into the forest.

At that conclusion of the ceremony, everyone sat up, and the elder asked each one in the circle to share what the experience was like. At her turn, Lynne told the story of her dream. When the elder heard about her dream, Lynne said that he gave her a strange look. Then her friend John said that he had experienced a similar vision.

When the elder had completed the ritual, he asked Lynne and John to remain. He told them that their vision was not a typical vision, but that they were being communicated with. They were being called, and they needed to respond.

John and Lynne talked after the elder left. Lynne was upset because none of this made any sense to her. It was an amazing dream, but she didn't know what to do with it – she just wanted to dismiss it.

John was very direct with Lynne: "I have had a lot of experience with the Shuar people of Ecuador, whose neighboring people are the Achuar. Lynne, the facial markings and headdresses tell me these are the Achuar people of the Ecuadorian Amazon." He explained that the Shuar had been in contact with what we call the modern world for thirty years. The Achuar had had almost no contact, but they had told the Shuar that their dreams and visions had revealed to them that contact with the modern world would inevitably come, but that it might come in a dangerous way. John said, "The Achuar are calling for us. I know who they are and where they are. I have wanted to take people into Achuar Territory for years. We have to go."

"No," Lynne said, "I have huge accountabilities in my work to end world hunger. My life is filled with critical commitments in Africa and Asia. I can't even get my arms around this. I have never been to South America. I don't speak Spanish. I know nothing about the Amazon. There's no way I can go to the Amazon with you."

They finished their work in Guatemala and agreed to talk again when Lynne returned from Africa. She flew directly to Ghana where she had a board meeting, and John went back to the Ecuadorian Amazon to work with the Shuar people.

Lynne's board meeting for The Hunger Project was in Accra, the capital of Ghana. She told me that she had been sitting at a large conference table, and that "all the faces around the table were Ghanaian – blue-black, as you know most Ghanaian people are. There were two women and seven men talking around the conference table.

"Suddenly, bright orange geometric face paint began to appear on the faces of the men. It was incredible. No one seemed to see it but me. Joseph, it's as if you and I were talking, and suddenly a banana began to grow out of your head, and we both just kept talking as if it weren't happening. If you saw it, and no one else said anything, you would think you were going crazy – as I did.

"I started to shake, so I excused myself and went to the lady's room. When I came back, everyone looked normal. They were still talking. Then it started to happen again – orange geometric face paint began to appear on the faces of the men. I really thought I was losing my mind. I was shaken and terrified. I excused myself, saying I was sick – which I actually thought I was."

Lynne then went upstairs to her hotel room, packed her bag, and caught the next plane back to San Francisco. On the plane, sleeping or waking, she saw the faces all the way home.

When Lynne arrived back in San Francisco, she shared the story with her husband, Bill, who was empathetic but sort of detached. "It was the only response he could have, she said. I had already begun to dismiss it and really didn't believe it had happened. But then I started to have dreams night after night that were exactly like the vision I'd had in Guatemala.

"Then the vision started showing up in the daytime. The final straw was when I was driving across the Golden Gate Bridge from San Francisco to Sausalito. Just as you get inside Marin County, you go through what is called the "Rainbow Tunnel." The visions started coming to me in the tunnel, and I couldn't see. I couldn't drive. When I got to the other end of the tunnel, I pulled over and just started to cry. Later, I talked to a therapist and tried all sorts of things, but the visions wouldn't go away."

She said she finally called John Perkins, who was still in Ecuador. There was no Internet back in 1994, so she sent faxes and voicemails to his home in Florida. Finally, when he returned home, he found not only Lynne's faxes but also faxes from his Ecuadorian friend and adventure travel partner, Daniel Koupermann, who had worked with him with the

Shuar. Daniel said he had paddled his canoe into Achuar territory with a Shuar indigenous man who protected him so that he could meet with the Achuar leaders. Daniel had been searching throughout the Ecuadorian Amazon, looking for a place to build a remote Eco-lodge in the rainforest and had begun discussions with the Achuar.

"The Achuar are reaching out to have people from the modern world come to them," he told John. "They want contact, and they want to initiate it. Come as soon as you can. They are asking for twelve people from the modern world to be the first they interact with. Here are the criteria: bring people who have global voices and open hearts, people who know that the rainforest is a crucial ecosystem for the sustainability of life. These people must respect the way of the Shaman and be ready to hear what the indigenous people have to share with the modern world."

Lynne and John then realized that they had to do this. Lynne took leave from her work with The Hunger Project and together John and Lynne organized a group of twelve people who met the criteria. Her husband Bill was her first choice, and a number of other very special people were included. They went to Ecuador and met with Daniel Koupermann, who led them on their journey to the Achuar.

"We flew to Quito," said Lynne, "and from there we traveled through the Valley of the Volcanoes, then down the eastern side of the Andes, down the Pistaza river canyon to the beginning of the Amazon basin, which stretches across the entire continent. We then flew in a military plane into Shuar Territory." At that point, a Shuar pilot took them, three people at a time, and dropped them off near a river in the remote Achuar Territory.

"Once all twelve of us got there," said Lynne, "it was starting to get dark. And then, there they were – the Achuar leaders with orange geometric face paint, and yellow and red feather crowns on their heads."

She said the Achuar put the twelve of them and their gear into canoes and took them to a camp – the site where the Eco-lodge was to be built. They met there for days.

Lynne said, "The Achuar elders did, to our knowledge, what no indigenous group has ever done: out of their deep concern for the growing threat to their ancient way of life and their recognition that the roots of this threat lay far beyond their rainforest home, they actively sought the

partnership of committed individuals living in the modern world." In
what was a monumental life-decision on their part, unthinkable before
this encounter, Lynne and Bill left their work to become the cofounders of
the Pachamama Alliance. *Pachamama* is a word from the native Quechua
language of South America, combining *pacha*, meaning "earth" or
"nature," and *mama*, the nurturing goddess of wisdom and spirit.

The population of the Achuar nation is about 6,000 people who
occupy nearly two million acres of pristine tropical rainforest in one of
the most biologically diverse regions of the world. The first initiative
of the Pachamama Alliance was to implement an integrated resource
management plan for the Achuar Territory, which was a great success.
The goal of this master plan is to ensure the long-term well-being of the
Achuar lands and culture.

"As I understand it," I said to Tahir as I finished the story, "Lynne's
experience mirrors the way Leroy Little Bear was 'seeing' us. When
you have access to that interconnected web of being, time and space
are irrelevant. You can *see* – call it 'remote viewing,' if you wish – and
sometimes you can even communicate."

Before Tahir could respond, David and Basil walked by, suggesting we
reconvene because Lee was preparing to present.

17. THE INNER STATE

[T]HE FACILITATOR WHO HAS DONE THE INTERIOR WORK WILL "SET THE FIELD"
FOR THE PARTICIPANTS AND HELP THEM LEARN THE WAY INTO THAT DEEPER
TERRITORY THROUGH DISCIPLINED PERSONAL PRACTICE. IT IS ONLY THEN THAT
PARTICIPANTS WILL BEGIN TO ACT AS A "SINGLE INTELLIGENCE" AND RELEASE
THE "PHENOMENAL CAPACITIES" ENFOLDED IN THE GROUP.

Earlier that morning at breakfast, Lee had told me that he had worked closely with Bohm from the early 1980s until Bohm's death in 1992. Lee wrote the forewords for a number of Bohm's books, including a book on the nature of thought and the self that was created from the transcription of a seminar Bohm held at Ojai – *Thought as a System.* (Lee had taught at Ojai with the noted Indian teacher, J. Krishnamurti, and was deeply involved in the dialogue groups that took place there. When I met Bohm in 1980, he spoke highly of Krishnamurti and suggested that Krishnamurti could help us create the Leadership Forum curriculum.)

I told Lee about my meeting with Bohm and that Bohm had shared with me an explicit mental model of the way he believed the world works and the way he believed human beings learn and think. To Bohm, it was clear that humans have an innate capacity for collective intelligence. They can learn and think together, and this collaborative thought can lead to coordinated action. We are all connected and operate within living fields of thought and perceptions. The world is not fixed, but is in constant flux; accordingly, the future is not fixed and so can be shaped. Humans possess significant tacit knowledge – we know more than we can say. The question to be resolved: How do we remove the blocks and tap into that knowledge in order to create the kind of future we all want?

By 1983, Bohm was devoting much of his time to exploring this issue of collective thinking and communication. Over the next eight years or so, a significant amount of progress would be made toward understanding this entire process, which Bohm simply called "Dialogue."

Beginning in 1985, Bohm put forward a series of propositions regarding a new vision for contemporary dialogue. This model of Dialogue received considerable attention throughout the United States, Canada, and Europe. Hundreds of formal and informal groups sprang up to practice it. Bohm's Dialogue model was also widely embraced by various organizational development and management communities, including Peter Senge's Organizational Learning Center at MIT. It deeply informed Peter's "fourth discipline," *team learning*. Team learning, Peter wrote, is vital because teams, not individuals, are the fundamental learning unit in modern organizations, and team learning starts with Dialogue – the capacity of the members of a team to suspend assumptions and enter into genuine "thinking together."

By the time I arrived in Boston in 1994 to work with Peter and his colleagues, there was a significant amount of excitement about Bohm's process of Dialogue. In 1989, Bohm had visited MIT and shared with Peter and his colleagues his view that true Dialogue could bring about a radical transformation of group consciousness and that under the right circumstances, "group mind" can develop and then access knowledge otherwise unavailable. Bohm felt the effect of such Dialogue could extend beyond the boundaries of the group, including subtle but significant effects within the organization itself.

That morning, after he had laid out this general background for those of us unfamiliar with it, Lee spoke of Bohm's intense hope for the transformative power of Dialogue on the collective mind. However, in his later years, Bohm felt that the impact of Dialogue seemed to have been erratic, even meager. In part, Lee felt, this lack of sustainability may have arisen from the commercialization of Dialogue whereby the training of facilitators was deficient, arising from an incomplete understanding of Dialogue itself as proposed by Bohm. Lee said that he wanted to focus on this one point – the way that Dialogue had been marginalized. In this way, he hoped to take a small step toward restoring certain essential features to their rightful place in Bohm's model.

Lee said that after Bohm had held seminars and meetings so that people could experience Dialogue, he had collected his thoughts in a small, self-published booklet, On Dialogue. It was intended primarily for distribution to those on the mailing lists of the Bohm seminars and sold, surprisingly, twenty thousand copies very quickly. This was a shorthand version of Dialogue – a pithy but incomplete extraction of the essential features of Dialogue intended for an audience already familiar with the deeper elements of the process, namely those who had attended the seminars with Bohm or read the detailed transcripts of the meetings. This incomplete version has been amplified in recent years through the publishers of several mass-market "how to" books. Taken together, the original incomplete booklet and the secondary materials have defined the field of Dialogue for an entire generation of practitioners.

What was missing, Lee said, was identified by Bohm in a conversation they had in 1992, shortly before Bohm's death: "People are not doing enough work on their own, apart from the Dialogue groups." Bohm and Lee concluded that facilitators and participants needed to do deep personal work on their own and then bring the fruits of that work back into the circle – and to do this work on a consistent basis. The "work on their own" would be contemplative practice – any form of meditation, mindfulness, or awareness training. Lee pointed out that when the mind is silent, transcending the ego (as it is during deep meditation), something beyond thought comes into operation – a conscious awareness that is *primary*. "It is an awareness decoupled from our view of our self or our view of the world. It is a genuinely new order of insight – a momentary loss of self in which we are nonetheless intensely aware." The point Bohm was making is that *if* the personal work is done, "the body is the individual gateway to a remarkable wealth of unexpected information."

Lee later told me a story about Krishnamurti that illustrates an aspect of what is meant by "work." He said, "At the very end of his life, Krishnamurti was involved in designing a study center in rural England, adjacent to the secondary school he had established there. The very heart of the building complex (both metaphorically and literally) was a meditation room. Krishnamurti died before the center was completed, but he gave some very precise instructions about how to use the room. 'Don't go to the meditation room to become quiet,' he said. 'Take quietness into the room when you go there.'

"This is really quite a profound view. It more or less upends all our views about *getting* something. It creates a very particular kind of non-presumptuous responsibility toward the world.

"Extended to group work, the implications are equally profound. Rather than going to the next Bohmian dialogue (or whatever the case may be) with an eye toward personal growth, or what I can get from it, I could go – having inwardly prepared myself – in a deep state of dynamic silence and 'give' that to the group work, right from the beginning. This of course does not preclude outward participation, but rather underlies it. I take total responsibility for the whole endeavor – inwardly, silently – and enter the group work with that sense of total responsibility. If multiple people in the group work understand this and actually do it, it will transform the group, and the work.

"I think this is what Bohm was alluding to when he said that people were not doing enough work on their own."

I found Lee's remarks highly instructive and remarkably relevant to the conclusions I had reached after my meeting in New York with Tex. There were two reasons for this:

First, I was grateful to have the "inside story" about the pamphlet *On Dialogue*. I must have read that little booklet ten times over the years since I had first seen it after arriving in Boston. Particularly, in the later years, I began wondering about the absence of a piece on the development of the "inner state" of both the facilitator and the participants as a necessary condition to Dialogue. Now I knew – and I felt a great sadness about the missing piece in view of the significant work that had been done on Bohmian Dialogue over the years. I was personally aware of a number of large-scale change efforts in Europe and America that had featured Bohmian Dialogue at the center of the process. None had reached their full potential because the need for these personal disciplines was not made specific.

Second, there were interesting parallels between this story and my growing realization that the U-process was being misunderstood and underutilized. The essence – the "little doorway at the bottom of the U" – had not been made explicit enough. The hard work of building capacity in the facilitators and the senior leaders of organizations has rarely been done. Just as in Bohmian Dialogue, the facilitator who has done the interior work will "set the field" for the participants and help them learn the way into that deeper territory through disciplined personal practice. It is only then that participants will begin to act as a "single intelligence" and release the "phenomenal capacities" enfolded in the group.

In his later years, Lee said, Bohm was fond of stating the maxim, "A *change of meaning is a change of being*." A number of participants at Pari mentioned this during the three days there. Lee and the others understood this to connote Bohm's view of a generative or creative order lying at the heart of the universe – a participatory universe. In such a universe, communion and fellowship are natural features of the topography, and intrinsic human warmth is common currency, part of the shared meaning of nature and society. Bohm felt the mind/body continuum ("You have to think with your whole body," he said to me) is concretely related to the deepest orders of the universe. If this is so, Lee said, then a change of meaning and purpose may open us to these orders, glimpsing a larger, perhaps very different universe.

Lee closed his remarks that day by saying that such deep reflections lie at the very heart of Bohmian Dialogue – not as a fad or theory, but as the deepest prompting of our humanity. And if this depth of Dialogue reemerges, it can contribute to a new and radical creativity, a collective intelligence that can beneficially affect the trajectory of our current civilization.

18. ENCOUNTERING THE AUTHENTIC WHOLE

WITHIN EACH PART IS ENFOLDED THE WHOLE, SO THAT EACH ELEMENT BECOMES A MICROCOSM OF THE MACROCOSM. IN THIS SENSE, THE INDIVIDUAL STANDS AS AN IMAGE OF A WIDER REALITY, WITH ALL ITS COMPLEX ORDERS.
— David Peat

When I had arrived at Pari, I had not been slated to be among the presenters; but before Lee presented, David and Tahir asked me to be first up on the last day. I was happy to do so because I wanted everyone there who had been so close to Bohm to know how indebted I was for all he had done for me.

I began my remarks by telling the group about my meeting with Bohm and what had happened with the Leadership Forum, with the scenario team I had led at Royal Dutch Shell in London, and with the Alliance Project and Innovation Lab, where we uncovered the U-process. I ended the brief "history" by mentioning the Global Leadership Initiative and the demonstration projects and drew a picture of the U-process as I now understood it, emphasizing the "little doorway" at the bottom of the U and the need for Stage IV facilitators – what I called "the advanced U-process."

The central point, I told them, is that I knew that none of this would have unfolded this way without Bohm's generosity of spirit. Here was a complete stranger calling Bohm's home on the Sunday his new book was announced. Everyone in the room knew how shy and retiring Bohm was. Yet, after just a short few words over the phone, Bohm changed his entire schedule and spent four hours with me the next day. It was an extraordinary act of *love*, I said – I knew no other word for it. And that single act of love and generosity changed the entire direction of my life, and of countless others. It also reflected the fact that Bohm was *living* what he was teaching – that there is a divine order to the universe, and that it's up to us to step into that "cubic centimeter of chance" when it is presented to us.

After I concluded my remarks, there was a stillness in the room. I felt the spirit of Bohm there, and I was filled with gratitude to David and Tahir for making it possible for me to be there and to heal the personal pain of not having flown back to London to be with Bohm after he had reached out to me in that letter.

Andrew was the first to comment. He was interested in the model of the U that I had drawn and how it could be used in organizational settings. After drawing a U model of the Innovation Lab, I told him the story of Gary Wilson's Los Angeles refinery and of Dave Chapman's lease-trading company. We talked about how one goes about selecting an organizational team to participate in an Innovation Lab. The guiding principle, I said, was that you choose a true representation of the whole system you intend to shift – a "strategic microcosm" of the whole.

Henri commented that this process aligned completely with the focus of all his work on the philosophy of Goethe's science. David agreed. As he put it in his book, *Synchronicity*, "Within each part is enfolded the whole, so that each element becomes a microcosm of the macrocosm. In this sense, the individual stands as an image of a wider reality, with all its complex orders."

When he reminded me of this at Pari, I said, "Exactly – the whole of the system is expressed or reflected in each person. Therefore, if we select a team that is truly representative of the organization, we have the whole organization in the room. The selection process begins with Deep Structured Dialogues, with the Generon interview team using their intuitive minds, deeply listening, reflecting, and inquiring, while nurturing attitudes of genuine openness and curiosity, and tapping people's genuine individual and collective aspirations. By diving into the concrete experience of the members of the organization, a picture of the whole begins to emerge. The interview team then reflects deeply together and comes up with its view of the whole system and who the best representatives will be."

"At a point during this generative interview process," Henri said, "a dynamic interior movement takes place and an accurate picture of the system becomes apparent."

Brian Arthur had described precisely the same process, which he used to understand a complex system and determine the best approach for an intervention. In our first encounter with Brian in Palo Alto, he had told us of his experience in Dusseldorf, Germany, as a summer intern with McKinsey & Company while he was a graduate student at the University of California at Berkeley during the 1960s. He described how his team was taught to understand the current reality of a complex system they were confronting:

> They just sat and sat. They didn't do anything. They just sat and observed and interviewed and observed and thought and went back and observed. It cost plenty to do this, but they were quite patient. This would go on for months until they had what I would now call a complex picture of what was going on – the opposite of what it would be to come in with some cognitive picture and say, "You need to be organized this or that way." They actually let a picture emerge. This wasn't lost on me. I would now call this an inductive rationality rather than a deductive rationality. Rather than laying a framework on top, they simply let the framework emerge.

Henri and I had a conversation at lunch in which I told him how much I respected his work on the philosophy of science and the perception of wholeness. He said that at one moment a year or so ago, he had experienced a sudden awareness "out of my heart" that "I am doing this work because of David Bohm – it all comes from Bohm."

19. PARTNERS IN EVOLUTION

IN DISCOVERING OUR OWN PURPOSE AND MEANING,
WE ENRICH MEANING IN THE UNIVERSE — WE CREATE SOMETHING
OF SIGNIFICANCE THAT HAS NOT BEEN THERE.

There was one final conversation that day that was of critical importance to me. As we finished talking about the advanced U-process and how powerful it can be when used properly, a protégé of one of the physicists raised the following question: "Yes, this process is robust, and the Lab team using it can manifest new realities – but what if it is used for evil? What if, for instance, a person with the mind of Hitler tried to employ the process?"

A very lively exchange then broke out, which lasted almost an hour. In the end, we went back to Bohm as the basis for the agreement we reached. Bohm wrote in *Unfolding Meaning* that meaning is an aspect of reality tied to the achievement of goals and to a specific context that is so subtle and complex that it cannot be represented by any closed formula. We inhabit a universe that is imbued with profound meaning. Wholeness, love, and significance infuse and inform the universe and give it shape and form. By its very definition, the advanced U-process is designed to access the Source and is also infused with meaning – truth and love are at its core, its essence. It is a process designed to bring forth the emerging reality *as it desires* – not as desired by people of ego or of mal-intent. In order to enable the collapse of boundaries between self, others, and the universe, one or a collective must *unambiguously* stand in a place of love, caring, and sacrifice for others – for the whole system under investigation. It is at this moment of oneness that the participants *are* acting out of the unfolding generative order – the unbroken wholeness from which seemingly discrete events take place. And it is at this moment that new realities are enacted for the benefit of the whole system. This is why the advanced U-process is so powerful. It is designed to serve life. The process itself is a volitional act of love, enabling new realities.

There is a well-known interview of Bohm by Renée Weber, a professor of philosophy at Rutgers, which describes the worldview advanced by Bohm that was at the center of the conversation that day in Pari. In that interview, Bohm said that there is profound and self-evident meaning infusing the universe. "It *is* its meaning – it doesn't have to have a reason." The meaning or end "could be said to be love – it could be said to be harmony."

Meaning is not final. We are continuously discovering it. And that discovery of meaning is itself a part of the reality. This worldview assumes a universal coherence and an all-encompassing principle that runs throughout the system at all levels. "We inhabit a universe that is alive with meaning and is conscious at all levels," Bohm told me.

Bohm thought that we could be actors in transforming reality through changing our meaning. "What we think and feel count. The key is the Socratic maxim: 'Know yourself – go inward and be observed.'"

After a long reflection on Bohm's words in this interview and his words to me in London, I concluded that in discovering our own purpose and meaning, we enrich meaning in the universe – we create something of significance that has not been there. We are part of it and it is part of us. *We are partners in the evolution of the universe.*

Bohm, David, and others there that weekend believe that "fragmentation of mind" has prevented most of us from holding this view of reality; it is what has blinded us to the creativity of the universe.

Bohm said to me in London that our tendency to see individuals and groups as "other" than ourselves has led to personal and social isolation, selfishness, and wars. David and others agreed that society and the individuals within it tend to operate in a rather mechanical way, responding to chance and new situations from relatively fixed positions and in uncreative ways. "They appear to be trapped in structures and forms of their own making, such as the beliefs, goals and values that have become so rigid that they are unable to move in the flexible and subtle ways that characterize the general order of the universe." In this process, the self rigidifies and becomes the supreme focus of attention.

20. SCIENCE AND HUMAN POSSIBILITY

WE'VE CONSTRUCTED THIS EDIFICE CALLED WESTERN SCIENCE, THAT
HAPPENS TO BE GOOD AT A FEW THINGS LIKE CT IMAGING OR GUIDING
SATELLITES OR DESIGNING NUCLEAR REACTORS, BUT IT DOESN'T MEAN
WE REALLY UNDERSTAND THE WORLD AT ALL.
– Brian Arthur

On the last morning before we all departed Pari, I had breakfast with
Jeffrey Tollaksen, chair of the Physics, Computational Sciences, and
Engineering Department at Chapman University, and his wife, Jayne. We
talked about the work he and Yakir were coleading at Chapman on the
reformulation of quantum mechanics, which was beginning to provide a
very different picture of the nature of time. *The Economist* characterized
this body of work by saying, "The good news is reality exists. The bad is
it's even stranger than people thought."

I told them of my continuing exploration of extraordinary human
functioning, particularly the capacity, individually and collectively, for
accessing tacit knowing, leading to the emergence of new realities –
discovery, creation, renewal, and transformation.

It turned out that Jeff knew all of the people who had helped guide me
over the years, including Willis Harman of Stanford Research Institute;
Larry Dossey, a medical doctor I had met in the 1980s; Rupert Sheldrake,
a British biologist I had worked with in London during the Shell years;
and Francisco Varela, a professor of cognitive science at the École
Polytechnique in Paris, whose work Jeff knew very well.

We talked at length about the frontier scientists who had followed
in Bohm's footsteps, developing Bohm's theories and proving new

ones. Jeff also told me about one of Bohm's colleagues whom he knew very well, Brian Josephson, the Welsh physicist who had become a Nobel Prize laureate at thirty-three years of age. Josephson was one of the better-known scientists who had studied the practical effects of Bell's Theorem of quantum nonlocality. He was now a retired professor at the University of Cambridge where he served as head of the Mind-Matter Unification Project in the Theory of Condensed Matter research group.

Josephson, Jeff said, had adopted the guiding principle, *nullius in verba* (take nobody's word), saying that if scientists as a whole denounce an idea, that should not necessarily be taken as proof that the idea is wrong; rather, one should examine carefully the grounds for that opinion and judge how well it stands up to detailed scrutiny. Josephson had written specifically on the work of Bell, demonstrating the existence of direct interconnections between spatially separated effects. Josephson's thesis was that Bell's Theorem may be put to use in very real, concrete, and practical terms. The existence of remote influences is suggested directly by experiments on phenomena such as telepathy (the direct connection of one mind with another) and psychokinesis (the direct influence of mind on matter), both of which are examples of extraordinary human functioning.

Jeff said both of these phenomena are often disregarded by orthodox science, but that the recent publications of important studies are causing these scientists to rethink their position. He suggested that I begin my further inquiry by contacting Robert G. Jahn, the Dean Emeritus of Princeton School of Engineering. He said he knew Bob Jahn well; that there was no more respected authority in the field than him; and that, in fact, he and Jayne had recently been in contact with Jahn and his research colleague, Brenda Dunne. Jeff gave me Jahn's coordinates, and that's where I began my final stage of exploring the state that Bohm, Varela, and all the others had described to me – "the state where we can connect deeply with others and doors open."

>─┼─◆>─O─<◆─┼─<

I left Pari after my breakfast conversation with Jeff and Jayne and drove to Florence where I spent the night before my flight home. I sat in my hotel room, reflecting on all that had occurred during the past several days. I committed to revisiting all my old research notes and books that informed my conviction that we live in an interconnected world and to contact Bob Jahn and Brenda Dunne – both of which I did immediately upon returning to my home in Vermont.

⊱┈✦┈○┈✦┈⊰

As I reflected on my experience in Pari, I was struck by the quality of conversation we had enjoyed there. Here was a collection of the most advanced minds in science; yet their presentations on some of the most complex and perplexing issues in modern physics were full of passion and expression – lyrical, like beautiful music, as Andrew had said. I was reminded of what Brian had said to us at Xerox PARC: "I've seen many, many things that I could not explain by . . . rational means." He said of science: "We don't know anything fundamental . . . it's a conceit to say science understands. It doesn't. It starts with a few magical unknowns. It starts with the unknown and labels part of it and knots a few strings below that and then hangs on to these strings – but they're not suspended from anything."

I found while going through my notes that Brian had commented on the evolution of complexity theory as a different way of seeing and conducting scientific inquiry:

> Complexity theory is really a movement of the sciences. Standard sciences tend to see the world as mechanistic. That sort of science puts things under a finer and finer microscope. In biology the investigations go from classifying organisms to functions of organisms, then organs themselves, then cells, and then organelles, right down to protein and enzymes, metabolic pathways, and DNA. This is finer and finer reductionist thinking. The movement that started complexity looks in the other direction. It's asking: How do things assemble themselves? How do patterns emerge from these interacting elements? Complexity is looking at interacting elements and asking how they form patterns and how the patterns unfold. It's important to point out that the patterns may never be finished. They're open-ended. In standard science this hits some things that most scientists have a negative reaction to. Science doesn't like perpetual novelty.

That day at Xerox PARC, Brian had said:

If you drill down deep enough into any subject, you get into philosophy. But philosophy is our way of coming to grips with the unknown. Philosophy isn't about the known. Philosophy is about the unknown. Philosophy is like scouts that we send out to explore new territory.

The point I want to make with all of this is we've constructed this edifice called Western science, that happens to be good at a few things *like CT imaging or guiding satellites or designing nuclear reactors*, but it doesn't mean we really understand the world at all. The only people who think we do are people who don't understand science. People like Bohm or Einstein, who really do understand science, will tell you that there is a thin layer of what we do understand, but down below or above it we don't know what we're in.

The Pari conversation had been imbued with the principle that "science was not certainty." Basil and others told me that Bohm was opposed to viewing science with certainty – that Bohm always spoke with humility and that his whole way of approaching anything, including life itself, was with wonder and full openness to any possibility. Basil said, "Bohm didn't give me answers; he just empowered me and opened the doors for me. He always empowered the listener to go on a journey of discovery."

⊳─◆─○─◆─⊲

One of the subjects that had run throughout my conversation with Bohm in London was what he called "the general fielding of all mankind." He said we are *all* connected and operate within living fields of thought and perception. "You can influence the field by your intention and way of being."

Just before returning to London in 1989, I had met Rupert Sheldrake, a British biologist who taught me much more about field theory. Rupert and Bohm met a number of times and often corresponded. Rupert felt their views of how the universe works were entirely compatible – for example, his idea of field consciousness, like Bohm's, suggested a continuum of nonlocal intelligence, permeating space and time. Rupert calls our "extended mind" a part of our biological nature.

Rupert's work suggests that the human capacity to enter into continuous subtle exchange with minds around us is shared with other species and that this feature of our mind is rooted in our evolutionary ancestry. His book, *Dogs That Know When Their Owners Are Coming Home*, tells of his analysis of dogs and cats that appear to know with uncanny accuracy when their owners are on their way home – no matter what the circumstances: whether at odd hours, unscheduled times, or after short or long absences. The cases strongly suggest that the animals are responding to their owner's *intention* to return home – an example of the "field phenomena" that led me to explore the scientific work done on remote viewing.

21. REMOTE VIEWING

HUMAN BEINGS HAVE A LATENT ABILITY
TO SEE ANYWHERE, ACROSS ANY DISTANCE.

My first introduction to the fact that human beings can connect with one another at very subtle levels of consciousness came from Willis Harman in the early 1980s during the Leadership Forum years and later at Shell in London in the early 1990s, when most of the information about the remote viewing work became declassified. When I met Willis in 1980, he had just been appointed as the President of the Institute of Noetic Sciences, founded by Dr. Edgar Mitchell, Apollo XIV astronaut and the sixth man to walk on the moon. For twenty or so years before that appointment, Willis had been a senior officer at Stanford Research Institute (SRI), a scientific think tank affiliated with Stanford University. He told me of the "remote viewing" studies that began in the early 1970s when various US government agencies (Department of Defense, Army, Navy, and others) initiated a research program at SRI. The experiments were pioneered by physicists Harold Putoff and Russell Targ.

The agencies wanted to determine if humans could "see" distant, strategically important locations through any known form of shielding. The studies examined the ability of humans to perceive objects and events at a distance, beyond the reach of ordinary senses. In these experiments, the "agent" would travel to a randomly selected, distant location while another person (the remote viewer, or person "perceiving") would remain in the lab, isolated from contact with anyone who knew where the agent had gone. At a designated time, the perceiver in the lab would try to describe where the agent was and what he or she was seeing.

The experiments showed that human beings have a latent ability to see anywhere, across any distance. An article about these experiments was published in the British journal *Nature* by Putoff and Targ and attracted criticism in the traditional scientific community. A subsequent movie, *Men Who Stare at Goats*, poked some fun at the "notion" of remote viewing. Over the years, I have had many occasions to experience comments from skeptics. I have come to understand that their skepticism derives largely from their unwillingness to reexamine their limiting belief systems. Yet detailed examination of the critiques of the journal article found that their authors were unable to explain away the reported results.

In 1988, a study was made of all the remote viewing experiments conducted at SRI since 1973. The analysis was based on 154 experiments consisting of more than 26,000 separate trials conducted over those sixteen years. The statistical result of this analysis indicated odds against chances of more than a billion-billion to one. Chance is not a viable explanation of such results.

The SRI studies were later refined and replicated by other scientists. The Princeton University Engineering Anomalies Research (PEAR) Lab conducted 653 formal remote viewing trials between 1976 and 1999. Bob Jahn and Brenda Dunne calculated that these experiments generated positive evidence verifying the SRI studies, with odds against chance at thirty-three million to one.

In telling me about the remote viewing studies at SRI, Willis said they originally used people who were known to have highly developed capacity for mental telepathy, but later, researchers used "ordinary people off the street." By a meaningful coincidence in 2001, just before we began to write *Presence*, I met one of the "highly developed" people with whom Willis had worked, and he gave me a personal demonstration of remote viewing.

>-+-+>-O-<+-+-<

My remote viewing experience began in early 2001, when I was in London meeting with Dadi Janki, a coleader of the Brahma Kumaris (BK), a seventy-year-old spiritual organization with close to a million members in a hundred countries. Dadi was accompanied by one of her key deputies, Sister Jayanti, who acted as interpreter since Dadi's first language was Hindi. Since the fall of 1997, I had attended an annual dialogue of thought leaders from across the world hosted by the BK's and Peter Senge to explore "the call of our time" – the collective responsibility we have at this time of fundamental change. A month earlier, I had been in Rajasthan for one of the dialogues, and Dadi had suggested I meet with her for a week to explore more deeply the pressing issues humanity faces.

We spent most of every day in deep dialogue. On the third day, Dadi excused herself to talk with one of her colleagues. Jayanti and I were engaged in light conversation, and I asked her if Dadi ever made public appearances to share her wisdom as she was doing with me.

"Oh, yes," Jayanti said. "She's done that from time to time; the last was a couple of years ago at Royal Albert Hall. She had a dialogue on stage with Uri Geller."

"Uri Geller!" I exclaimed. "I've heard about him. I'd love to have a conversation with him; I'd learn a lot about the very subject of the book we're about to write."

About that time, Dadi Janki returned, and I mentioned to her what Jayanti and I were discussing. Dadi listened and confirmed how interesting it was to make that presentation with Geller. As we turned to our dialogue, she said, "But we haven't been in contact with Uri for two or more years."

We resumed our dialogue, but about five minutes later, the phone rang and Jayanti picked it up. Neither Dadi nor Jayanti were very happy about this; they had left strict instructions for us not to be disturbed. We paused while Jayanti spoke to Dadi's assistant: "But we left firm instructions not to be disturbed. Who is it? . . . Oh." She covered the mouthpiece of the telephone, looked at Dadi and said, "It's Uri Geller. He insists on speaking to you."

I almost fell out of my chair. Dadi sighed.

Jayanti said, "I think you'd better take it."

Dadi picked up the receiver and said, "Hello, Uri. . . . Yes. . . . I'm in dialogue. . . . No, we can't be disturbed." She listened a few moments and then said, "Ok, Uri. Come to the old house at 7:00 p.m. We will have finished our meditation and you can meet him then."

Dadi said, "Uri wanted to know with whom we were talking. He said it was important he meets you. So I made arrangements. This might inform your work." The synchronicity was, to say the least, startling. They, however, didn't seem very surprised, and so we returned to our dialogue.

At around 6:00 p.m., we went to the small home where the BK London operation had started over twenty years previously. As agreed, after our meditation, Geller arrived and was escorted into the room. After Uri and I got acquainted, Dadi suggested we all talk and that Uri and I could have dinner at the BK University dining room later.

So Uri and I went together to the large, empty dining room at the university where I was staying and sat down to a long and deep conversation over dinner. Almost immediately, we determined that Willis Harman was a mutual friend. Geller had worked with Willis, Hal Putoff, Russell Targ, and the other scientists at SRI during the remote viewing studies from late 1972 until early 1975.

One thing led to another, until Uri offered to demonstrate remote viewing to me. He suggested I take two pages from my writing pad. He asked me to draw the most original and complex design I could imagine on my sheet. Once I completed it, I was to look at it and concentrate on the drawing. He said he would replicate it on the sheet I gave him. He went to the other side of the dining hall and we turned backs to one another as I began to draw. I was completely alone on the opposite side of the large room from him.

I was both interested and amused by the opportunity to experience this small demonstration. I was vaguely aware that Uri was a controversial figure, and there were many who were skeptical of his psychic ability. Yet, based on what Willis had told me, I suspected he would indeed "see" my drawing and reproduce it – a classic "remote viewing" or picture-drawing experiment that Willis had told me about. What I didn't anticipate was this: once I had finished the picture, he came over and showed his own version to me. It was, of course, the same. I smiled. And then he suggested I pick my page up, put mine and his back-to-back and go over to the nearby floor lamp. He suggested I look "through" the two pages. I did so; and *they were precisely the same!* There was not a millimeter's difference in the two drawings. That, I told him, was really surprising.

Then, after we talked a while longer, I began asking him about psychokinesis (or "telekinesis" as it's sometimes called) – the capacity he had demonstrated many times to audiences. I told him I was aware of the experiments involving mental interaction with random number generators and the fact that elite athletes had spoken about their ability to "see the ball into the receiver's hands" in American football, or "see the ball into the hole" in golf. We spoke about Bohm and the questions he had raised with me at the outset of our conversation twenty years ago in London about "what is mind, and what is its relationship to matter?"

It was getting late. As we were walking toward the door, we passed by a table where a few young people were still sitting. He said, "Come here – I'll show you something." He picked up a large spoon off the table, held it in the palm of his hand, and stared intently at it. Within seconds, the spoon started to bend, curling up into a "U." As this started to happen, he put the spoon in the palm of my hand. The spoon continued to curl up in my hand, palm up. The "bottom of the U" where the spoon was bending was very warm to the touch – almost hot. He smiled and gave me the spoon to keep. He said he hoped we could stay in touch in the future; we exchanged contact coordinates and said goodbye. I have that spoon in my library today.

22. THE POWERFUL NATURE
OF HUMAN INTENTION

*WE HAVE THE CAPACITY TO EXTEND OUR OWN COHERENCE INTO THE
ENVIRONMENT THROUGH OUR INTENTION AND WAY OF BEING.*

During this time of reflection and research, I wrote to Dr. Jahn and
Dr. Dunne at Princeton, telling them of my meeting at Pari and that
Jeff and Jayne had strongly suggested I meet them. We agreed to have a
conference call – and the first one led to several more.

In one of the early calls, I asked them for a reading list of reference
material on the work they had done over the years, particularly on the
effect of nonlocal consciousness – human intention acting on physical
reality. I was particularly interested in the studies they had conducted in
the PEAR Laboratory that Jeff had told me about.

They told me that Jahn had established PEAR in 1979 to pursue
the rigorous scientific study of the interaction of human consciousness
by using sensitive physical devices, systems, and processes common to
contemporary engineering practice. During a span of over twenty-five
years, they had retained an interdisciplinary staff of engineers, physicists,
psychologists, and humanists to conduct a comprehensive agenda of
experiments and had developed complementary theoretical models to
enable a better understanding of what Bohm had spoken to me about
and what we had considered in Pari – the role of consciousness in the
establishment of physical reality.

Jahn and Dunne suggested a list of some thirty papers and books
about their work at PEAR and were kind enough to send some of them
to me. I began absorbing everything they sent to me and mentioned.

In the process I found a special issue of *Explore* that was devoted
entirely to the work of PEAR. It was an anthology containing the peer-
reviewed publications, technical reports, and papers that had flowed
from the program since 1979. That volume gave me a good overview
and explanation of the extraordinary work of PEAR; and I found it of
particular interest because the lead article in the volume was by a good
friend of mine, Dr. Larry Dossey.

▷─┼─◁▷─○─◁▷─┼─◁

I had first met Larry in 1983, when I visited Dallas to consider opening
an American Leadership Forum chapter there. The mayor and a number
of the business and community leaders in Dallas had gathered, and as I
made my way around the large room, I went over to Dossey, not knowing
who he was, and introduced myself. We spoke for a moment or two, and
out of the blue I brought up Bohm's name. It turned out that Dossey was
a devoted student of Bohm's, having read *Wholeness and the Implicate
Order* and other papers by and about him. From that moment, we had an
important connection, and since then I have relied on him for advice and
direction as I pursued my search to understand more about extraordinary
human functioning.

At the time I met Larry, he was chief of staff of Medical City Dallas
Hospital and had helped establish the Dallas Diagnostic Association, the
largest group of internal medical practitioners in the city. He had been
a battalion surgeon in Vietnam, where he had been decorated for valor.
Over the years, we discussed how battlefield conditions enable greater
collective consciousness.

In 2000, when we were conducting the research for the Alliance
Project, I took Otto with me to spend a half-day with Larry and his wife,
Barbara. I'll never forget one particular part of that interview, when we
were talking about the collapse of boundaries between self and others and
how new realities arise. I asked, "Where does the willingness to risk your
life for someone come from?"

"Why one human being would actually put his life on the line for
another one has always puzzled me," Larry said. "When I got back from
Vietnam, I read Joseph Campbell's *Power of Myth*. Campbell talked about
an essay Schopenhauer wrote in which he asked the same question: 'What

is it that makes one individual in a situation of crisis or danger actually willing to give their life for another individual?' His answer was that *at that moment, they're not two people; there is only one*. So this person is not saving another person. This person has identified so completely that he no longer is separate from the other individual."

Over the years, Larry became more and more interested in the role of the mind in health and healthcare, publishing nine books and numerous articles on the subject. The primary quality of all his work is scientific legitimacy and an insistent focus on "what the data shows." As a result, his colleagues in medical schools and hospitals all over the country trust him and often invite him to share his insights. He has lectured all over the world, including at major medical schools and hospitals – Harvard, Johns Hopkins, Cornell, and the Mayo Clinic. The impact of his work has been remarkable. Before his book *Healing Words* was published in 1993, only three US medical schools had classes devoted to exploring the role of prayer in health; currently eighty medical schools have initiated such courses, many of which utilize his works as textbooks. He introduced the concept of "nonlocal mind" as an emerging image of consciousness. It was for all of these reasons that I found Larry's opening article in *Explore* so interesting.

Larry's article gave an overview of the PEAR studies and why they are so important to human welfare. The PEAR team, in examining how consciousness manifests, has produced, he said, the largest database of its kind in the world, using random number generators (RNGs). RNGs are computer programs that generate numbers that meet statistical conditions for randomness, as required for various research applications. Because the RNGs are tested regularly to be sure they are shielded from electromagnetic, telecommunications, and all other sources of electronic interference, any deviation from the normal 50/50 chance "heads and tails" is significant rather than the result of a systematic bias.

In twenty-seven years of PEAR studies, participants – who are ordinary people, not highly gifted psychics – have been able to affect the random movement of the number generators *simply by their remote intentions – their acts of will*. So long as the participants willed the machine to register heads or tails, he or she had some influence on it a significant percentage of the time.

If you combine all the studies into a "meta-analysis," as two of the scientists at PEAR have done, the odds of this overall score occurring are a trillion to one.

Dossey said, "The sustained ingenuity, precision and courage demonstrated by the PEAR team in examining how consciousness manifests may be unparalleled in the annals of science – in its ambition, audacity and reach, exceeding even the Manhattan Project."

After reading and rereading all the technical reports and peer-reviewed articles in the *Explore* volume and after reading material on Jahn and Dunne's reading list, I concluded that the scientific studies irrevocably confirm Bohm's "unbroken wholeness" of the universe. This was, I thought, an important step in my search for understanding. We have the capacity to extend our own coherence into the environment through our intention and way of being.

23. COLLECTIVE COHERENCE

*THIS [STUDY] SUGGESTS THAT WHEN MILLIONS TO BILLIONS OF PEOPLE
BECOME COHERENTLY FOCUSED, THAT THE AMOUNT OF PHYSICAL
COHERENCE OR ORDER IN THE WORLD ALSO INCREASES.*
– D. I. Radin

Before I met with Jahn and Dunne, Generon had an opportunity to
work with one of their key scientists at PEAR, Dean Radin. Susan Taylor
and I were working with a senior team at a global pharmaceutical firm
codesigning a U-process Innovation Lab. The design team met for three
days with a number of scientists and thought leaders from various fields,
focusing on human transformation. Radin was among those; he prepared
over a hundred PowerPoint slides reflecting the essence of his work
over his professional career. He had worked with Willis at SRI on the
remote viewing program, with Jahn and Dunne at PEAR for a number
of years, and at AT&T Bell labs and GTE laboratories on advanced
telecommunications systems. He has conducted research on extraordinary
human functioning for almost two decades. His two books, *The Conscious
Universe* and *Entangled Minds*, are highly regarded by peer researchers and
theorists.

During our many telephone conferences and his presentations to us,
Radin described what are known as "field consciousness studies," a term
coined by Roger Nelson at PEAR during the mid-1990s. The essence
of this research is to determine whether the behavior of a group can
influence the output of an RNG (random number generator) and under
what circumstances it may do so. The technology today has allowed
scientists to build extremely accurate portable RNGs. Researchers
took these portable RNGs to places where groups were engaged in an

activity calling for highly focused attention, as in meditation or Bohmian
Dialogue. Such field experiments have been conducted since about
1995 in the United States, Europe, and Japan. Over a hundred of these
experiments have taken place, reflecting that groups do in fact appear
to be capable of influencing nearby RNGs. They were conducted at
theatrical performances, scientific conferences, Native American rituals,
Japanese festivals, sports competitions, and live television broadcasts.

The findings were so striking that in 1997 Nelson began an
international research project called the *Global Consciousness Project*
(GCP). Nelson and his colleagues created an Internet-based, worldwide
network of RNGs. By 2005, sixty-five RNGs located around the world
were engaged in a continuously running field consciousness experiment.
Their output is collected continuously and fed via the Internet to
computers in which the data is stored and analyzed. By April 2005,
Nelson and his international consortium of scientists had analyzed
almost two hundred events of global interest, including natural disasters,
New Year celebrations, terrorist activity, large-scale meditations, sports
events, outbreaks of war, and tragic deaths of well-known figures and
celebrities. Many showed the predicted influence registering on the
network.

By far, the most dramatic events analyzed were those of September 11,
2001, when the RNGs around the world behaved in highly nonrandom
ways. The GCP Network registered the single largest drop for any
day in 2001. The GCP team published their findings in the journal
Foundation of Physics Letters. According to their analysis, the minute-
by-minute behavior of the statistics across the global network matches
the chronology of the terrorist attacks, with the nonrandom behavior
beginning around 5:00 a.m. and peaking around 11:00 a.m. Eastern (US)
Daylight Time, staying extremely deviant into the evening, with odds
against chance of a million to one. Radin said to us, the team believed the
nonrandom behavior was the change in humanity's collective attention
that day.

Referring to the project's work from August 1998 through April 2005,
Radin concluded, "This suggests that when millions to billions of people
become coherently focused, that the amount of physical coherence or
order in the world also increases." Roger Nelson concurred:

> We do not have a theoretical understanding of the sort that
> must underlie robust interpretations . . . but I would like to
> describe a speculation . . . that the instruments have captured
> the reaction of a global consciousness. . . . The results from this
> scientific study are an apparent manifestation of the ancient
> idea that we are all interconnected, and that what we think and
> feel has an effect on others.

>—⟨•⟩—○—⟨•⟩—⟨

At the conclusion of this time of deliberation, I formulated the first
two of what eventually became four principles. These two reflected all I
had learned since my first meeting with Bohm in London in 1980.

1. **There is an open and emergent quality to the universe.**
   A group of simple components can suddenly reemerge at a higher
   level of self-organization, as a new entity with new properties.
   We can't find a cause or reason for this emergent quality, but as
   we experience it again and again, we see that the universe offers
   infinite possibility.

2. **The universe is a domain of undivided wholeness; both
   the material world and consciousness are parts of the same
   undivided whole.**
   The totality of existence is enfolded within each fragment of
   space and time – whether it is a single object, thought, or event.
   Thus, everything in the universe, including human intentions and
   ways of being, affects everything else, because everything is part of
   the same unbroken whole.

Although I was satisfied with what I had concluded, two important
questions remained for me: What is the Source of our capacity to access
the knowledge for action we need at the moment? How can we learn to
reliably enable that capacity individually and collectively?

24. THE SOURCE OF REALITY

THERE EXISTS AN ETERNALLY CREATIVE SOURCE
THAT LIES BEYOND THE ORDERS OF TIME.
– F. David Peat

In November 2008, I went to Princeton to spend the day with Jahn and Dunne. I had spoken with both of them over the telephone many times, so all of the preliminary introductions had been made, and we had a good deal of knowledge about each other and our work in the world. For most of the day we met at Bob's home, where he did most of his writing since retiring from Princeton. Like Bohm, Bob possessed impeccable credentials: Professor Emeritus of Aerospace Sciences at Princeton University and Dean Emeritus of its School of Engineering and Applied Science. He served three consecutive five-year terms as dean and directed major research programs in advanced aerospace propulsion systems for over forty years with ongoing sponsorship by NASA, the Air Force, and various industrial firms. He directed the PEAR Laboratory for twenty-eight years. He spoke to me with great precision and authority, yet, like Bohm, his countenance was one of deep caring and love for his work and its implications for society. He was a man of great heart.

Brenda Dunne was a developmental psychologist (formerly at the University of Chicago), who directed and supervised the full spectrum of PEAR activities and oversaw the research projects of visiting scholars and student interns. It was clear to me from the outset that Brenda was utterly devoted to Bob and his life's work. She, like Bob, was a perfectionist about detail. And, not surprisingly, she too was a person of high passion and complete commitment to the realization of their work for society.

We spent much of our time exploring the essence of their work, and I confirmed that Bob and Brenda's worldviews were completely aligned with those of the scientists in Pari. The vast array of the inexplicable effects that emerge from the PEAR studies, they said, stem from one understanding of reality where "mind and matter meld." The effort, they said, now needs to focus on how to access and utilize "this ineffable, primordial Source."

The balance of our conversation that day had the same quality as my conversations with Bohm in London and Brian Arthur at Xerox PARC – I knew I was being given a gift of unspeakable proportions. I can only describe my state as one of *grace* – receiving in clear and unmistakable terms the precise understanding and overarching framework I had been seeking for so long. Here is my effort to summarize the conclusions I drew from their view:

- Human knowledge processing is not completely executed within the physiological brain. Rather, the brain is one neurologically localized utility that serves a much more extended individual "mind" or "consciousness."

- The information exchanged between the Source and the individual mind (consciousness) is continuous, but is heavily filtered, allowing the mind only tiny glimpses of the grand complexity and scope of the true, ultimate order that exists.

- We are capable of establishing dynamic dialogue and resonant channels of communication with the Source – passing information into the Source, as well as extracting information from it. This can be accomplished with practice and discipline, enabling communication between mind and the Source that exceeds conventional expectations.

- Our channels for reception can be tuned to allow and to amplify the information exchange.

These six features are essential to enable enhanced communication with the Source:

1. **The Power of Perspective:** Openness to alternative perspectives; the possibility of alternative realities; or, in Michael Ray's terms, suspending and letting go of old mental models and our own internal voice of judgment. This requires a strong act of will to deviate from the security of the traditional collective belief system.

2. **The Magic of Metaphor:** Utilization of transdisciplinary metaphors to shift the perceived context of the task at hand from a context in which the task seems impossible to one where it is possible, even if unlikely. For example, remote perception "receivers" have described one tactic as staring at a blank screen, waiting for a movie to begin.

3. **The Role of Resonance (Love):** Unambiguously standing in a place of service, self-sacrifice, and love. This is Martin Buber's "I and Thou" relationship, where two previously separate "I's" comprise a shared "we" that can change the perception and interpretation of reality. This shared "we" alters the definition of self (as Lee Nichol pointed out), which results in an enhanced dialogue with the Source and an increased probability of physical events arising from the Source.

4. **The Use of Uncertainty (Surrender):** Avoiding perceived attachment to the outcome of the process, choosing instead to "flow" with the indeterminacy itself. As Buber says, "Bring it to reality as *it* desires," instead of as "I" desire.

5. **The Case for Conceptual Complementarity:** The great physicist Niels Bohr proposed that the wave-particle dualities appearing in atomic-scale physical interactions could be rationalized only by regarding these two modes of behavior not as contradictory, but as "complementary," in the sense that each displayed a legitimate interaction, and both were necessary to specify the phenomenon completely. Similarly, in connecting to the Source at the bottom of the U, an individual or a group must hold a strong intention to manifest a new reality, yet, at the same time be willing to manifest the new reality "as it desires." Jahn and Dunne say, "The

ultimate pair of complementary conjugates, of course, is that
of Consciousness itself and the ineffable Source in which it is
immersed, and with which it intersects to generate all manner of
experience. Despite their vast disparity of character and function,
it is they who comprise the universe of life, and they who are the
parents of all reality."

6. **Inner Self-Management:** Use of internal tools for self-
   transformation. I have had an opportunity to explore this
   domain with Willis Harman, Francisco Varela, the scientists at
   Pari, Brian Arthur, John Milton, Dean Radin, and William A.
   Tiller, who was chair of the Department of Material Sciences
   and Engineering at Stanford University. All agree, as do Jahn
   and Dunne, that techniques like meditation, qigong, and yoga,
   wherein one stills the mind, increase access to the Source. Any of
   these practices create a state of alternate consciousness and tune
   our channels of reception, amplifying our information exchange
   with the Source. Metaphorically speaking, it is as though we are a
   radio, and our bandwidth expands, allowing us to be receptive to
   a larger number of wavelengths in the field.

⊱—◦—⊰

After I returned home, I began recording in my journal the importance
of the day I had spent with Bob and Brenda. The following day, I began
searching for passages I had read earlier that spoke about the mind/matter
dialogue and the manifestation of new realities.

I found two sets of passages that were utterly aligned with what
Bob and Brenda had said. The first, which was not surprising, was from
David Peat's *Synchronicity*. In that book, David said that humans and
nature form an indivisible whole and that there is a bridge between the
perceived two worlds of mind and matter. Our inner world is one of
mind and spirit: direct experience, love, loss, art and music, spirituality
and numinosity. Our world of matter and energy is one of physics,
chemistry, elementary particles, and quantum fields. But as Bohm, Peat,
and the other physicists in Pari saw things, these were two sides of *one
reality*.

I read and reread David's book, which I found absorbing not only because it tracked what I'd learned from Bob and Brenda, but also because it expressed my precise experience at moments of connecting to the Source. I summarized what I learned from the book in six major points:

- There exists an eternally creative Source of infinite potential that lies beyond the orders of time. It exists before the sequential orders of time and is found beneath the levels of increasing subtlety from which the orders of mind and matter emerge. It is the one underlying Source constantly giving birth to the universe at every eternal moment. It is the wellspring of the universe itself.

- Within this process of emergence, each moment contains the present and the seeds of the future – within each process of nature is enfolded the whole.

- Within the creative moment, explicate and implicate, mind and matter are indissolubly linked. The creative energy that is let loose at this moment can be compared to that released in a nuclear reaction, when the internal structure of the nucleus is rearranged. Energy is directed to new possibilities. The future and its endless possibilities become open to creative change.

- If the human subject does not possess the honesty of mind and purpose to see things as they really are (interconnected and full of meaning), creativity is blocked, and the patterns of the present will continue to unfold into the future.

- There is an art to "knowing" the significance of a particular moment of time, the seed from which future events will flow. We perceive this moment not consciously, but through our tacit or primary knowing and then we can take right action in the moment.

- Within quantum theory is the notion of the "strange attractor," which is an expression of all the interactions and relationships within a complete system and its environment. It exerts a subtle influence so that the system weaves and dances around it, relatively free, yet never escaping from its influence. When

we take "right action" at the proper moment in time, those
with similar intention and purpose are drawn to us, creating the
phenomenon of "hidden hands" and "doors opening."

Thinking about these ideas, I was reminded of my meeting with the
cognitive scientist Francisco Varela in which he had described what
happens to those to attain the state of "authentic presence" – "we exert
an enormous attractive power, and if others are in that same space or
entering it, they resonate with us, and immediately doors are open to us.
It is not strange or mystical. It is part of the natural order. . . . This state
is there waiting for us. . . . All we have to do is to see the oneness that we
are."

25. FORESIGHT

HUMAN CONSCIOUSNESS IS ABLE TO EXTRACT INFORMATION
FROM PHYSICAL ASPECTS OF ITS ENVIRONMENT BY MEANS THAT ARE
INDEPENDENT OF TIME AND SPACE.
– Robert Jahn

Robert Greenleaf, the originator of "Servant Leadership" – one of
the most influential business concepts of our time – called foresight "the
central ethic of leadership." "To see the unforeseeable" and "know the
unknowable," Greenleaf said, is the mark of a leader.

At the very heart of all I have written in *Synchronicity* and *The
Red Book* is the notion of sensing and actualizing emerging future
opportunities *before* they have manifested. The conversations in Pari and
later with Bob, Brenda, and Dean Radin, were all infused with the notion
of "knowing" that transcends both time and space. Indeed, an accepted
principle running throughout all I've learned over the years about primary
knowing, or knowing from the Source, is that it lies beyond the orders
of time. Given the essential importance of future knowing to this whole
inquiry, at every opportunity during my meetings with these remarkable
people, I made it a point to focus specifically on this domain – the human
capacity for *foresight*. Some of what I learned about our gut and our heart
as a gateway to foreknowledge was astonishing.

Bob was explicit with me: "Human consciousness is able to extract
information from physical aspects of its environment by means that are
independent of time and space." Brian Josephson, the Nobel physicist,
said, "So far, the evidence seems compelling. What seems to be happening
is that information is coming from the future." Radin said that when you
step back from all the research and studies, what you find is "a spectacular

body of converging evidence indicating that our understanding of time is seriously incomplete. These studies mean that some aspect of our mind can perceive the future. Not infer the future, or anticipate the future, or figure out the future. But actually *perceive* it."

Larry Dossey has spent years examining case studies and the research of the most respected scientists of the twentieth century. In *The Power of Premonitions*, he reveals the world of science and research that proves the human capacity for knowing the future. "We do not have to wait for scientists to endorse unbounded, infinite, non-local minds," he writes. "They have already done so."

"Compelling laboratory evidence that we have an innate ability to sense the future has been growing quietly for nearly two decades," writes Dossey. "It has been gathered primarily by . . . Dean Radin. . . . Radin has found that our central nervous system automatically responds to events that have not yet happened and of which we are unaware in the present. His findings are perhaps the most serious challenge ever mounted to the assumption that our consciousness can only access the past and present." Radin showed the results of these particular experiments to us in 2008, while we were preparing for a U-process Innovation Lab.

Radin designed experiments to evoke an emotional response using randomly selected, emotionally arousing or calming photographs. Indicators of autonomic activity included skin conductance level (SCL) and photoplethysmographic measures of heart rate and blood volume. Comparison of SCL response between emotional and calm trials showed a significantly greater change in electrodermal activity approximately five seconds before viewing an emotional picture than before viewing a calm picture. "In other words, the participants 'pre-acted' to their own future emotional states *before* the emotional pictures were seen, and before the computer had selected them." Radin called this faculty "presentiment," to indicate a prior sentiment or feeling.

To date, there are thirty-eight replications of the presentiment study, from labs in a half-dozen countries, and overall the results show a strikingly robust effect. "It's difficult to overestimate the value of this line of experimentation," Dossey says, "and as Stanley Krippner, the prominent psi (psychical) researcher, states, these studies suggest that presentiment actually does reflect foreknowledge of future events. In my opinion, this is currently the most important experiment in psi research."

Jahn and Dunne conducted 653 formal remote viewing trials between 1976 and 1999. These studies showed that spatial separation is not an important factor: the same degree of success is seen whether the agent and the percipient are in the same city or whether they are separated by thousands of miles. Interestingly, neither does *time* matter. Bob and Brenda explained to us that in most of their trials, the receiver "saw" the information from the agent precognitively – up to several days *before* it was sent, and *before* the image had been randomly selected from the target pool. They referred to these experiments as PRP, or precognitive remote perception. For example, in the case of an agent looking at the Danube River and transmitting this view to the percipient, the percipient, at a distance of 5,600 miles from the agent on the Danube, correctly identified it as the location, more than twenty-three hours *before* the agent was actually at the Danube's edge.

The verbal descriptions by the percipients in these PRP studies were remarkable in their similarity to the corresponding photographs, and some represented virtually photographic precision. Bob and Brenda explained that over the course of the studies, the percipients' perception ranged in accuracy from virtual precision (like some of those above) through varying degrees of correspondence with the components and ambience of the scene, to total irrelevance. Of the 334 PRP trials that were published as of 1987, final odds against chance for the PEAR researchers overall database were 100 billion to one.

The PEAR studies have been replicated by many different investigators, including Harman's SRI and Science Applications International Corporation (SAIC) in La Jolla, California. "The odds against chance in the SRI data are a billion billion to one. These results have been published in scientific journals such as *Nature*, *Proceedings of the IIE*, and the *Journal of Scientific Exploration*," Dossey notes.

26. ACCESSING THE SOURCE – THE SURPRISING ROLE OF THE HEART

*THE INTUITIVE MIND IS A SACRED GIFT AND THE RATIONAL MIND
IS A FAITHFUL SERVANT. WE HAVE CREATED A SOCIETY THAT HONORS
THE SERVANT AND HAS FORGOTTEN THE GIFT.*
– Albert Einstein

In my attempts to understand how best to access the Source, I learned that the "intuitive *mind*" is potentially present not just in the brain, but throughout the body. Complex neuronal structures exist throughout the body, particularly in the heart and the gut. Some researchers even talk about the "little brain in the heart." One of them is Bruce Cryer, CEO of HeartMath LLC. The work of HeartMath involves measuring the impact of consciously accessing what HeartMath calls "heart intelligence." There is compelling evidence that the body's perceptual apparatus is continually scanning the future and that the heart is involved in processing and decoding intuitive information.

I first met Bruce and Doc Childre, the founder of HeartMath, in 2000 at the beginning of the research project for the Alliance. Bruce and Doc have achieved global recognition for their work in harnessing the power of the heart-brain connection. They and their team of research scientists have developed practical, scientifically validated methods and groundbreaking products designed to increase individual workplace performance while reducing stress. Their training programs and techniques are being used by Fortune 100 companies, hospitals, police academies, and schools on four continents to achieve better business outcomes, including employee retention, reduction in health costs, and increased performance, both in creativity and productivity.

When I first met Bruce, he said, "Intelligence in the human system is far more distributed than we used to think. The old model that the brain was the master computer and everything else followed its commands is wrong. We're saying the heart is a highly intelligent system, although nowhere near as neurologically complex as the brain. It produces hormones and neurotransmitters that we used to think were only produced in the brain. The heart affects brain function in many ways – electrically, biochemically, etc. Biologically, there's compelling evidence to suggest the heart is an intelligent system."

In that same meeting, we learned that heart and gut intelligence have also been demonstrated at a cellular level. The implications of this are far-reaching. Bruce explained that neurochemicals, the carriers of nervous-system information, are produced in vast quantities in the gut and the human heart. These chemicals in turn affect brain processing and virtually every other organ in the body.

For several years, he said, researchers have studied the enteric nervous system, which is a complex set of nerves found in the intestinal tract. This elaborate network of neurons and neurochemicals is so sophisticated and complex that it is now called the "gut brain." Its activity directly affects brain function. More neurons exist in the gut – about one hundred million – than in the entire spinal column.

And, he continued, new research has been published showing that a sophisticated intrinsic nervous system is now known to exist within the human heart. Neurochemicals such as norepinephrin and dopamine, formerly believed to be produced only in the brain and nervous system, are also produced within the heart, as well as hormones such as ANF, known as the balance hormone.

These appear to directly affect brain function. Just as the gut brain's circuitry allows it to act independently, learn, remember, and produce "gut feelings," so the existence of the heart's brain may help to explain the wide range of feelings associated with the heart. So it appears that at least three brains – mind, gut, and heart – are networked together, influencing each other twenty-four hours a day, much of it below our conscious awareness.

Bruce told us that day that it is important to see the heart for what it is – the source of our core power and essential in helping us to access new intelligence: "In a sense, the physical heart is the transmitter station of spirit. Many cultures throughout history have considered the heart to be the core of the soul, even the core of intelligence. It's really only been during the last hundred years in Western civilization that the heart has not been viewed to be a source of intelligence. In most other cultures of the world, the heart is still seen as central to what the experience of being human really means."

He said that evidence is mounting that the heart's intelligence is a core operating system in the human being, capable of the coherent organization of mental, emotional, and cellular intelligence. Mental intelligence, he said, is to analysis as heart intelligence is to intuition. The management of one's emotional nature, including the ability to generate positive emotion, provides the gateway for unleashing intuition.

"One of the key insights that has shaped our research over the last fourteen years was the suggestion that intuition is a type, or bandwidth, of intelligence central to the design of the human being. We are suggesting that the human system is preprogrammed to operate with a high level of operational intuitive intelligence, and that in this accelerated information age we have created the perfect conditions to optimize it."

In 2004, experiments by HeartMath, led by researcher Rollin McCraty, extended Dean Radin's presentiment findings. McCraty and his team showed emotionally arousing or calming pictures to twenty-six subjects who were experienced meditators or skilled in emotional management techniques taught by HeartMath. The HeartMath subjects showed a significant presentiment effect in the behavior of the heart. About five seconds before viewing a randomly generated image on a computer screen, the subject's heart rate pattern would begin to change to reflect, in advance, whether the image would be stressful or calm. The heart "knew" what lay ahead, even though the subjects were alone in the room and had no conscious knowledge of what image would appear.

The researchers also produced evidence that the heart may perceive future events *before* the brain does:

> . . . recent work in neurocardiology [suggests that] the heart is
> a sensory organ and an information encoding and processing

center with an extensive nervous system, enabling it to learn, remember, and make functional decisions *independent* of the cranial brain. . . . The body's perceptual apparatus is continuously scanning the future. The heart is directly involved in the processing of future emotional stimulus seconds before the body actually experiences the stimulus. . . . What is truly surprising about this result is the fact that the heart appears to play a direct role in the perception of future events; at the very least it implies that the brain does not act alone in this regard.

The report concluded:

Although our finding that the heart is involved in intuitive perception may be surprising from one perspective, it is worth noting that in virtually all human cultures, ancient and modern, the heart has long been regarded as a conduit to a source of information and wisdom beyond normal awareness. Thus, our data may be seen as providing scientific evidence for an intuitive capacity that humankind has known and used for many millennia."

The HeartMath researchers had reached the same conclusion as the physicists at Pari and as Jahn and Dunne. Here is the way they reported it:

Assuming these psychophysiological effects continue to be demonstrated in future research, they are strong evidence for the idea that intuitive processes involve the body accessing a field of information that is not limited by the constraints of space and time. More specifically, they provide the compelling basis for the proposition that the body accesses a field of potential energy – that exists as a domain apart from space-time reality – into which information about "future" events is spectrally enfolded.

The report concluded with the following language:

The investigation of intuitive perception promises a rich harvest for humankind: an enlarged scientific understanding of human perception and consciousness, and even a new view of ourselves and of our relation to the material and nonmaterial worlds. In this rapidly changing and highly complex world of ours in the twenty-first century, we believe there is a critical role for intuitive perception in informing choice and decisions in virtually every aspect of human life. It is through scientific research, such as this, that we can build an understanding of how and under what conditions intuition occurs, and thus also learn the keys to harnessing and developing its power.

Although the language may differ, in every instance I've encountered, I've heard the same basic conclusion: that there exists an eternally creative Source (the field of active information) that lies beyond the orders of time, enfolded in an implicate or nonmanifest state, constantly prepared to give birth to manifest reality – the explicate order – at every moment. Human beings are exquisitely designed to sense the future, shape it, and bring it to reality – to actualize it when necessary and meaningful, as *it* desires.

But what about sensing the future *together* in groups? I was eager to learn what science had to say about this possibility.

27. GROUP ENTRAINMENT

REGULAR INTERACTION WITHIN A COHERENT GROUP SHOULD AMPLIFY THE
HARMONIC RESONANCE OF THE GROUP'S ENERGETIC FIELD WITH THE ENERGETIC
FIELD OF AN OBJECT OF ATTENTIONAL INTEREST.

— Bruce Cryer

In May, 2008, during a workshop we conducted for a senior leadership
team, I spent a day in further conversation with Bruce. In addition to
describing to the group HeartMath's research on future knowing, he
spoke at some length to them about a series of studies that are yielding
interesting findings that confirm our own experience in Innovation Labs.
Their research teams have studied the amplifying effect of working in
teams that are highly aligned or "entrained."

Entrainment is the scientific term for the synchronization of systems.
Flocks of birds, schools of fish, and the pacemaker cells in the human
heart are all examples of entrainment. Teams that are entrained function
smoothly, capitalizing on the creativity and intelligence of the individual
members with minimal distortion or static. Examples, Bruce told the
group, are sports teams, music groups, and dance troupes who perform "in
the zone," who achieve a high level of entrainment and move effortlessly
as one coherent whole without sacrificing individual excellence and
uniqueness.

The principle HeartMath has learned is that complex systems
such as teams require coherent individual parts to attain new levels of
coherence as a whole. As the team members become more self-managed
and internally coherent, communication distortion is reduced, and the
system entrains. Once entrained, a jump to a new level of effectiveness is
possible.

The self-management Bruce spoke of is of the same quality Bohm and Lee Nichol focused on – meditation, yoga, qigong, or HeartMath's process, "quick coherence" through "heart focus, heart breathing, and heart feeling." Over the years, HeartMath has measured the effectiveness of teams' pre- and post-coherence training. In one study, he showed us that creativity rose, for example, from 68 percent to 82 percent, and efficiency rose from 48 percent to 80 percent.

What would be of great interest to the group we were training, Bruce said, is that their research reflected that a coherent group gains *amplified access* to "the field" as opposed to a group that is not entrained. The work done by a Lab team in the days before a wilderness solo is an exercise in group entrainment. When the group returns from solo to collaborate on the common endeavor, it is in a state of high entrainment, and its capacity to access the Source is greatly amplified. As Bruce put it to us that day:

> Regular interaction within a coherent group should amplify
> the harmonic resonance of the group's energetic field with
> the energetic field of an object of attentional interest. This in
> turn will strengthen the signal the individuals receive from the
> field of nonlocal intuitive information. This should produce
> stronger intuitive ability than when the individual is operating
> in isolation.

28. THE POWER OF
PASSIONATE ATTENTION

*THIS EXPERIENCE OF AN IMMEDIATE, TOTAL SENSE OF THE THING
AS A WHOLE IS QUITE UNLIKE THE INFORMATIONAL PROCESSING
EXPERIENCE OF NORMAL AWARENESS.*

In that last workshop with him in 2008, Bruce told us of the studies the HeartMath team were conducting that year with a team of researchers from the Australian Graduate School of Entrepreneurship (AGSE), which confirmed the 2004 results in the trials described earlier that were led by McCraty. The AGSE-HeartMath studies sought to explain the success of repeat entrepreneurs. Based on presentiment studies (this time using a roulette wheel and comparing serial entrepreneurs, ordinary business people, and unsuccessful entrepreneurs as the participants) and studies conducted in 2006 and 2007, the teams affirmed the earlier findings; but in these investigations "the pre-stimulus difference reflecting a nonlocal intuitive effect (was) 12–14 seconds before the betting outcome was presented to the participants."

Bruce said these studies are moving the teams significantly closer to a large-scale field study on "nonlocal intuition" in which a statistically adequate sample of repeat entrepreneurs is compared with samples of unsuccessful entrepreneurs and ordinary business people. All of the evidence so far shows that the repeat entrepreneurs have a greater ability to perceive and process nonlocal information about potential business opportunities than unsuccessful entrepreneurs and the ordinary businessperson.

The team's hypothesis is that the entrepreneur's passion and highly focused attention directed to the future business opportunity attunes

135

their body's psychophysiological systems (brain, heart, and autonomic nervous system) to "a domain of quantum-holographical information, which contains implicit, energetically encoded information about the object."

They further concluded, based on these studies, that nonlocal intention is sensed by the entrepreneur and perceived in the body and mind "as a certainty" about the "thing" yet to happen. This thing can be, for example, a mental construct such as a thought or idea. Often the feeling is one that is *absolute*, experienced as beyond question or doubt – and the feeling can encompass positive emotion, such as optimism and excitement. "This experience of *an immediate, total sense of the thing* as a whole is quite unlike the informational processing experience of normal awareness. In normal awareness, the contents of the mind are updated incrementally, as in moment-by-moment sequences of sensory experience unfold."

Relying, in part, on the research conducted by William Tiller, the Stanford physicist with whom we had worked earlier that same year, the research teams found that the entrepreneurs' ability to sense the future was enhanced when these subjects calmed their minds and feelings and adopted "a heart-focused state of positive emotion directed to the object."

The findings of the AGSE-HeartMath team and their conclusions about the "source of intuitive information," the role of risk-it-all intention, and the quality and delivery of the information (absolute certainty and arriving whole vs. incrementally) conforms precisely to my direct experience and to the studies, research, and evidence I had gathered over the years.

>-+-◆>-0-<◆-+-<

Reflecting on all I had learned from my second passage in Baja with John; from my time in Pari at the Bohm symposium; from the conversations in Princeton with Bob and Brenda; and from my own research, I formed the third principle:

3. There is a creative Source of infinite potential enfolded in the universe.
Connection to this Source leads to the emergence of new realities

– discovery, creation, renewal, and transformation. We are partners in the unfolding of the universe.

During the later part of my visit with Bob and Brenda, we discussed two matters that set the course for the next stage of my journey: first, that organizations must pay attention to the deep Source of knowledge from which profound innovation occurs; and second, that organizations must develop core practices that inspire creativity and action.

But how could such organizations be developed? And what core practices would allow leaders to draw from the infinite potential of the Source? The answers to those questions were slowly revealed to me through a series of deep dialogues I had with Kaz.

29. CONNECTING TO THE SOURCE

THE FUTURE HAS AN ANCIENT HEART.
– Carlo Levi

My dialogues with Kaz began in the summer of 2009 in my home in Stowe, Vermont, while Susan Taylor, Kaz, and I were forming plans for the continuation of a partnership he and I had begun fourteen years earlier. These dialogues drew deeply from Kaz's years of training as a transpersonal psychologist and from his years working with Scott Peck, who had written that Kaz demonstrated "extraordinary creative genius" in forming a state of community while working with businesses in large-group settings. In this work, Kaz was able to promote unitive states of consciousness – the collapse of boundaries Bohm spoke to me about in London and that occur "at the bottom of the U," leading to profound individual and collective insights and breakthrough solutions.

Kaz and I had coauthored a paper in 1998 with Peter Senge called "Setting the Field: Creating Conditions for Profound Institutional Change" – later known at SoL as "The Field Paper." The Field Paper, based on all we'd learned about the subject over the past twenty years, was deeply informed by Bohm's understanding of the way the world works. We had concluded the paper by saying, "We believe this process could represent the beginnings of a major breakthrough for large-scale transformative change, and we sincerely hope that this paper will challenge others to think and explore along similar lines."

> However, what fundamentally distinguishes the approach does not lie in its explicit activities, but in its intent and assumptions, starting with a particular view of reality. We

believe that behavior throughout large organizations is influenced by subtle fields of thought and emotion, and that these fields are susceptible to change – indeed, they are continually unfolding. We believe the awareness of such emerging fields lies at the heart of all true leadership. Reality is not fixed but continually in flux. True leadership is the art of working with emerging fields to bring forth new realities.

Though radical in contrast to many contemporary prescriptions for leadership behavior, this view of leadership is not new. Seventy-five years ago, philosopher Martin Buber said, "What is to come will come only when we decide what we are able to will." Buber went on to make a subtle distinction between two sources of will: our "unfree will that is controlled by things and instincts" and our "grand will." Human beings cultivate this grand will over their lifetime through developing the capacity – as Buber put it – "He listens to what is emerging from himself, to the course of being in the world; not in order to be supported by it, but in order to bring it to reality as it desires."

Far from being an abstract ideal, we believe that leaders at all levels can cultivate this listening and that doing so transforms an organization's capacity to create its future.

Although we were unable to express it with precision then, when we wrote of Buber's "grand will," that phrase served as a placeholder until we began to simply refer to "the Source" and to "cultivating the capacity to access the Source."

⊷⊶⊙⊷⊶

During our dialogues, Kaz introduced to me to *heuristic discovery*, a method of inquiry based on Michael Polanyi's work, which seeks to create knowledge using reason, intuition, and, significantly, passion. With Dean Brown as his mentor, Kaz had spent years continuing Polanyi's investigations into the tacit dimension of scientific discovery. Later, Kaz took a family-owned enterprise in Los Angeles from a Stage II organization to an emerging Stage IV company using a process of discovery strikingly similar to the U-process.

Because of these experiences, Kaz was immensely helpful to me as I was confronting the question of how organizations can develop core practices to enable their people at all levels to connect to the Source, enabling superior performance. During these conversations, I told Kaz

I was generally aware of Polanyi's work through my conversations with Ikujiro Nonanka during the Salon in 2000, but that I had never read his books. Kaz recommended three of Polanyi's books – *The Tacit Dimension, Meaning*, and *Personal Knowledge* – and also prepared written memoranda for me on specific topics using material from these books and from his dissertation.

After absorbing this material, I realized that Polanyi's work was central to the answers I was seeking. It describes the foundation for Nonaka's process theory of the knowledge-based firm; it is directly aligned with and descriptive of Brian Arthur's process of advanced decision-making and of solving "the most complex issues" facing any organization; and it corresponds to the advanced version of the U-process that I had been developing.

Of immense importance is Polanyi's idea that the successful process of knowledge creation explicitly and necessarily rests on its normative nature. That is, as the scientists at Pari, Princeton, and HeartMath asserted, the foundation of the discovery of knowledge that changes the world as we know it indispensably rests on the values, passion, and meaning assigned to the project by the innovators. In our knowledge-based economy, where knowledge is the most important resource, superseding the traditional resources of land, capital, and labor, a deep understanding of this process is vital to any organization.

Polanyi's intellectual journey was extraordinary in its reach. Long before his books on knowledge creation were written, Polanyi had become well known across the world as an extraordinarily innovative scientist, particularly in physical chemistry. He published his highly acclaimed first paper, on the chemistry of hydrocephalic liquid, when he was only nineteen. After establishing his leading role in the world of the natural sciences, in the late 1940s, he made a shift to focus on the social sciences and wrote a series of influential books on economic, social, and political issues from his chair at Manchester University in the UK.

The third stage of his journey (built on these first two) was to attempt to understand the world – physical as well as mental – through the perspective of *knowledge creation*, drawing on his personal experience and the ideas and analysis presented by scholars in a wide range of fields over hundreds of years. The three books mentioned above all bear directly on the subject of tacit knowing and were written in the eighth decade of Polanyi's life.

Polanyi's concept of tacit knowledge or tacit knowing were most fully expressed in the 1951–52 Gifford lectures at the University of Aberdeen, which were published as *Personal Knowledge* in 1958, and in the 1962 Terry lectures at Yale University, which were published as *The Tacit Dimension* in 1966. Polanyi regarded the "structure of tacit knowing" as his most important discovery. In *Personal Knowledge*, he claimed that the human mind is led to discover orders that go far beyond his rational understanding – "his triumph lies precisely in his foreknowledge of a host of yet hidden implications, which his discovery will reveal in later days to other eyes." He referred to this hidden knowledge as "ineffable knowledge" and as "supernatural knowledge," which he described as "tiny fragments of the universe embodied in man." He referred to the process of such innovation as the "actualization of certain potentialities" lying dormant in the universe.

This view of the way the universe and our world unfolds is remarkably aligned with that of David Bohm's "implicate order," Brian Arthur's "access to deeper knowing," and Bob Jahn and Brenda Dunne's "ineffable, primordial Source." The ideas advanced in Polanyi's lectures were not only far-reaching and important, but also astonishing in that they were published almost twenty years *before* Alain Aspect's confirmation of Bell's nonlocality theory.

30. THE STRUCTURE OF
KNOWLEDGE CREATION

*THE DISCOVERER WORKS IN THE BELIEF THAT HIS LABORS WILL PREPARE HIS MIND
FOR RECEIVING A TRUTH FROM SOURCES OVER WHICH HE HAS NO CONTROL.*

Polanyi talked about "the advancement of knowledge that cannot be achieved by any application of explicate modes of inference, however diligent" or "by the diligent performances of any previously known procedure." Polanyi calls this "heuristic inquiry." *Heuristic* derives from the Greek *heuriskein,* to find or discover. The "nature of discovery" – knowledge creation – is the root subject that animates Polanyi's philosophy.

In his three books, Polanyi wrote about the path anyone – scientist, creative artist, entrepreneur – takes in the process of actualizing a hidden potential or creating new knowledge. I say "anyone," because over the last thirty years, I've conducted in-depth interviews with over 100 entrepreneurs and innovators in commerce, science, economics, education, government, and nongovernmental organizations, and I know that these discoverers would all recognize Polanyi's description as applicable to their own inner states, the actions taken from these states, and the results achieved.

I read Polanyi's beautiful words with great care because they describe exactly what it *feels like* to discover new knowledge. To clarify my own thinking, I summarized Polanyi's description of this path into six stages:

1. **Solitary Intimations Arise**
   The process of discovery begins almost indiscernibly as solitary intimations of a problem to be discovered. These are faint voices

from within – an "un-specifiable impulse" in which one senses a problem others do not notice as even existing. Bits and pieces are sensed, offering faint clues to a hidden potential. These are only fragments of a possible coherent whole that guide the sensing of the problem and the decision to inquire.

2. **Emergence of Heuristic Passion Driven by Universal Intent**
   The initial vague intimations give way to a firm decision by the discoverer to inquire. This develops into a calling, a *heuristic passion* that is driven by *universal intent*, the act of surrendering to something greater than oneself. The choice to take this journey is an existential choice – the discoverer becomes fully committed to the undertaking as an aspect of reality. The stakes are high. Great hazards lie ahead in the risk of time, money, personal prestige, the loss of one's self-confidence, and the risk of defeat. "The discoverer has chosen to stake, bit by bit, his entire professional life." In the face of this peril, the discoverer crosses the threshold engaging his destiny, his "vital design," what he is here in this world to do. He undertakes this passionate pursuit of a hidden meaning, guided by an intensely personal *foreknowledge* of this hidden reality.

3. **Surrender and Sense of Service**
   The discoverer seeks to detach from his or her current knowing in order to access more deeply what is seeking to manifest. This is a process that must continue throughout the journey. The lonely discoverer is "continually drawn to surrender false knowledge" in order to access more deeply what lies beyond current understanding. The whole undertaking is in the nature of what Polanyi calls a *fiduciary act*. The choices made in the cause of the inquiry are responsible choices:

   His vision of the problem, his obsession with it, and his final leap to discovery are filled from beginning to end with an obligation to an objective properly called *external*. His acts are intensely personal acts, yet there is no self-will in them. Originality is guided at every stage by a sense of responsibility for advancing the growth of truth in men's minds. Its freedom lies in this perfect service.

4. Indwelling as a Dynamic Force of Comprehension

The discoverer works in the belief that his labors will prepare his mind for receiving a truth from sources over which he has no control. He works night and day in "intense, absorbing, devoted labour," immersed in the experience. He lives in the undertakings, surrendering himself to the work, absorbed in the inherent quality of the experience for its own sake, dwelling within a framework of inherent excellence. "We dwell in the hope that we may, by the grace of God, be able somewhere, somehow, to do that which we must, but which we can at this moment see no way to do. . . ."

5. Retreat and Sudden Illumination: The Gift of Grace

"(T)he quest is brought to a close after a quiet interval (when the efforts of the imagination are at a rest), by a sudden illumination which offers a solution for the problem. Such an event is purely spontaneous and so may be called the work of a 'concluding intuition'. . . . (T)here is always the same story over again. . . ." Polanyi says it is axiomatic that true discovery is not a strictly logical performance. There is a gap between the antecedent knowledge from which the discoverer started and the consequent discovery at which he arrives. "Illumination" is the leap by which the logical gap is crossed – " . . . here we have, in paradigm, the Pauline scheme of faith, works and grace. The discoverer works in the belief that his labours will prepare his mind for receiving a truth from sources over which he has no control. I regard the Pauline scheme, therefore, as the only adequate conception of a scientific discovery." Such illumination may come as a surprising confirmation of a theory during the course of pursuing possibilities suggested by existing knowledge. It may also come while pursuing radically novel discoveries that depart in some deep sense from what went before. In either case, once having received such illumination, " . . . I shall never see the world again as before. My eyes have become different; I have made myself into a person seeing and thinking differently."

6. Testing and Verification

Such a "flash of triumph" usually offers no final solution, "but

only the envisagement of a solution that has yet to be tested.
. . . Thus, both the first active steps undertaken to solve a
problem and the final garnering of the solution rely effectively
on computations and other symbolic operations. . . . However,
the intuitive powers of the investigator are always dominant and
decisive."

There is a singular power in Polanyi's description of discovery. The
process rests on a clear view of how the universe works: innovators have
the power to actualize hidden potentials in the universe, *but* they must
be guided by "an intensely personal foreknowledge of this hidden reality."
Every step of the process depends on this "personal foreknowledge" that
the solution exists, but is not yet known. The discoverer's worldview
is paramount. They see the universe as Bohm and the scientists at
Princeton and Pari see it: a world made up of the explicate order (what
is already manifest) and the implicate order (that which lies hidden and
unmanifest). It is the implicate order (the Source) that holds infinite
potential – the hidden possibility or solution that is being sought.

This principle was explicitly pointed out to me at Princeton.
The second of Jahn and Dunne's six features, "Enabling Enhanced
Communication with the Source," is the requirement that the
participants shift the context of the task at hand from one that seems
"impossible" to one of "attainable possibility."

31. THE RELEASE OF LIMITING BELIEF SYSTEMS

BY *DELIBERATELY CHANGING THE INTERNAL IMAGE OF REALITY, PEOPLE CAN CHANGE THE WORLD. INDEED, THE REAL FUNDAMENTAL CHANGES IN SOCIETIES HAVE COME ABOUT NOT FROM DICTATES OF GOVERNMENTS AND THE RESULTS OF BATTLES, BUT THROUGH VAST NUMBERS OF PEOPLE CHANGING THEIR MINDS.*
— Willis Harman

The drive to learn and know our fundamental nature is a basic human need. I now realize that this need kept drawing me to understand the fundamental aspects of my direct experiences of primary knowing. There were missing pieces to the "whole" I just couldn't articulate. Sometimes I felt I was coming close to knowing – I was gaining tacit knowledge, but I couldn't give voice to it. But when I met with the scientists at Pari and Princeton and later read Polanyi's precise description of the way radically new knowledge is discovered, everything suddenly came together for me.

Over the years, my worldview had shifted. I had released my limiting belief systems, which had been inculcated in me over a lifetime, and discovered that a profound shift had occurred in my metaphysics – my philosophy of being and knowing.

Metaphysics formats and enables experience and, in turn, molds scientific, social, and individual reality. It provides a description of human experience that satisfies a deep longing within us. Dean Brown, in answer to the question, "What is the use of metaphysics?" replied, "We become what we behold."

Willis Harman once said to me, "By deliberately changing the internal image of reality, people can change the world. Indeed, the real fundamental changes in societies have come about not from dictates of governments and the results of battles, but through vast numbers of people changing their minds."

I have learned over the years that Stage II leaders and even many Stage III leaders operate under obsolete assumptions and inner mental models of which they may no longer even be aware. These limiting belief systems inhibit leaders at all levels from pursuing and discovering novel opportunities. The result is repeated strategic failure even in enterprises that are exceedingly well run.

32. SUDDEN ILLUMINATION

In his book, *Cosmic Law: Patterns in the Universe*, Dean Brown wrote that Polanyi's "sudden illumination" was an invariant law of the universe. He said that what is presently concealed will eventually be revealed and that revelation comes through grace alone. Revelations can be progressive and can take place in science, self-knowledge, and learning. One knows one is on the right track if the revelation is progressively more beautiful.

Brown uses the word *metanoia* to describe the experience of sudden illumination or revelation. "For the Greeks, it meant a fundamental shift or change, or more literally transcendence (*'meta'* – above or beyond, as in 'metaphysics') of mind (*'noia,'* from the root *'nous,'* of mind). In the early (Gnostic) Christian tradition, it took on a special meaning of awakening shared intuition and direct knowing of the highest of God."

"No amount of . . . logic . . . can bring you to this 'aha' experience," writes Brown. "It just comes when it comes, and brings with it certainty. . . . Moses had a revelation of this sort when he encountered the burning bush on Mount Horeb."

In science, this "aha" experience occurred to Leonard Euler in 1773 when he found the relationship $exp(i*pi) = -1$. This has sometimes been called the most beautiful expression in mathematics. A similar revelation occurred to Charles Hermite in 1859 when he discovered that $exp(pi*\sqrt{163})$ is almost an integer. Similarly, "Many of the great masterpieces of art and literature were felt by the artist to have been 'dictated' by a higher agency."

In the history of science and discovery, the role of the sudden insight is a recurring theme. It happened to Archimedes – as he was taking a bath, he came upon a way to calculate density and volume. While lying in a bed, watching flies, René Descartes realized he could describe a fly's position by what is now known as coordinate geometry. A popular story goes that in an orchard, when he saw an apple fall, Sir Isaac Newton formulated what became his law of universal gravitation.

I've spoken with Brian Arthur many times about this phenomenon of sudden illumination. One day during a retreat in Montana, he regaled me with story after story about the discovery of radically new technologies or radically novel discoveries in science and economics. His own influential "theory of increasing returns" – which offered a paradigm-changing explanation of why some high-tech companies achieve breakaway success – came while on a two-month leave in Hawaii when "instantaneously I realized I had something important in economics. This is the 'bottom of the U.' The insight arrives whole . . . and it arrives with a 'knowing' that the solution is right – a feeling of its appropriateness, its elegance, its extraordinary simplicity. . . . And it arrives not in the midst of activities or frenzied thoughts, but in moments of stillness."

I asked Brian where he thought such origination came from. He paused a moment and said, "We can't rule out spirit." Then he paused again, smiling, and said, "Let's just call it grace."

Two of America's best-known discoverers, Thomas Edison and George Washington Carver, were highly explicit in describing the source of their knowledge. Edison, considered an atheist, believed the wellspring of his knowledge to be "the infinite forces of the Universe." He wrote in 1911, "People say I have created things. I have never created anything. I get impressions from the Universe at large and work them out, but I am only a plate on a record or a receiving apparatus – what you will." His wife once commented, "He believes that his inventions come *through* him from the infinite forces of the Universe – and never so well as when he is relaxed."

George Washington Carver discovered a remarkable number of uses for peanuts and their chemical derivatives and displayed an outstanding degree of creativity in other aspects of his life. When he was asked what methods he used when confronted with a problem, he replied, "I never grope for methods. The method is revealed the moment I am inspired to create something new." He also spoke more specifically, saying, "When I touch that flower, I am not merely touching that flower. I am touching infinity."

33. ANCIENT ANTECEDENTS

WHEN WE CONNECT TO THE SOURCE . . . PERCEPTION
ARISES "FROM THE WHOLE FIELD."
– Eleanor Rosch

Long before Western scientists acknowledged the field of active information, the zero-point field, or the implicate order, ancient scholars and indigenous healers described the "web of creation" in the words of their traditions. The Hopi spoke of the "web that unites the universe." Many of the earliest creation myths invoke a primordial state or ground out of which all nature emerges. This is at the heart of John Milton's teachings in his *Way of Nature* passages Brian Arthur introduced me to. The prayers of the Tibetan Buddhists, dating to the fourth century, speak of a field that unites all things. Throughout history, scientists, mystics, poets, and artists have attempted to describe aspects of the creative Source.

As civilizations developed, myth gave way to natural philosophies, which, in turn, ultimately gave way to modern physics. Bohm defined the implicate order to me as "the unbroken wholeness out of which seemingly discrete events arise. All of us are part of that unbroken whole, which is continuously unfolding from the implicate and making itself manifest in our explicate world." David Peat devoted an entire chapter in *Synchronicity* to the subject of "The Creative Source."

Eleanor Rosch named the attributes of primary knowing: "timeless, direct, spontaneous, open, unconditional value, and compassionate." She said all of these attributes go together and constitute one thing, what some in Tibetan Buddhism call "the natural state" and what Taoism calls "the *Source*." "When we are connected to that Source, things become

more integrated . . . with intention, body and mind coming together.
. . ." When we connect to the Source, she said, perception arises "from
the whole field. The notion of 'field' was the closest thing I could come
up with in our current sciences to describe this phenomenon."

Rosch's reference to Taoism led me to read all I could find on the
subject of the Source as described by the Taoists. For me, the *Tao Te
Ching* was the most accessible and informative; and the translation by R.
L. Wing, *The Tao of Power*, was, by far, the most revealing and useful.

Wing says that no one actually knows where the *Tao Te Ching* came
from; but this slim volume of about five thousand words forms the
foundation of classical Chinese philosophy. According to legend, the book
was written by Lao Tzu, a gifted scholar who lived twenty-six centuries
ago and worked as the custodian of the Imperial Archives during the reign
of the Chou Dynasty. Lao Tzu presented to the ancient world a collection
of strategies and attitudes designed to bring true influence and power to
leaders and personal freedom to those whom they led. The *Tao Te Ching*
– *The Tao of Power* – has remained in print for 2500 years and has been
translated more frequently than any other classic except the Bible.

According to Wing, the *Tao Te Ching* explores an evolving force
called *Tao* that operates throughout the universe and lies latent in every
individual. *Tao*, precisely translated, means "the way the universe works."
Te is a term that refers to the potential energy that comes from being
aware of and aligned with the forces of nature – from being in the right
place and in the right frame of mind at the right time. *Te* describes the
personal power that comes from being in step with the Tao. The Tao can
be thought of as an evolving force that operates throughout the universe.

Another translator of the *Tao Te Ching*, Lionel Giles, says:

> Never, surely, has so much thought been compressed into so
> small a space. Throughout the universe there are scattered a
> certain number of stars belonging to a class known as "white
> dwarfs." They are usually very small, yet the atoms of which
> they consist are crushed together so closely that their weight is
> enormous in relation to their size, and this entails the radiation
> of so much energy that the surface is kept at a temperature
> vastly hotter than that of the sun. The *Tao Te Ching* may fitly
> be called a "white dwarf" of philosophical literature, so weighty
> is it, so compact, and so suggestive of a mind radiating thought
> at white heat.

I read passages from Wing's book over and over again, coming to appreciate the way the *Tao Te Ching* hinted at the nature of the universal energy, Tao, by describing what it is not. Awareness of this universal force cannot be reached through the ordinary senses – it cannot be seen or heard or felt. It resides in the realm of the intuitive mind and can be perceived only through its effect on the physical environment and on ideas, events, and social transformation.

Wing notes that Lao Tzu believed that intuitive knowledge was the purest form of information:

> In the *Tao Te Ching*, he compels us to use intuition as an equal partner with logic, and encourages us to combine our cognitive understanding of the world around us with a strong personal vision. . . . In this way, we gain a holistic and precise view of reality because we are also perceiving mood, change, and possibility – the mood of the times, the changes as the society evolves, and the possible future we might create. It is the view of the artist, the philosopher, the visionary – a view that has always carried with it the power to influence the world.

As I sought to understand the more subtle aspects of knowledge creation, I found the symmetry between what Lao Tzu said and the words of the theoretical physicists I had encountered over the years to be extraordinary and deeply satisfying. The philosophy that Lao Tzu left behind suggests an experiment, one that individuals undertake when they are ready to enter the next phase of human evolution – that of fully conscious beings who are directing their own destiny and the destiny of the world around them.

It began to dawn on me that I was also seeking a verification of my own direct experience of these subtle realms – most often experiences that occurred in nature.

34. NATURE AND SACRED SPACES

IN THE WILDERNESS, SELF-REALIZATION IS BORN, AND, OVER TIME, IT CAN MATURE INTO A DISTINCTIVE KIND OF AWARENESS, WHICH HAS BEEN DESCRIBED IN THE ANCIENT TEXTS FOR THOUSANDS OF YEARS.

From my earliest memory, I always experienced the power of nature – but I've always struggled to explain this experience to others. In developing the curriculum for the Leadership Forum, we all simply took it as gospel that the wilderness experience would be at the heart of the year-long program, enabling the injunction Bohm gave me to break the "self-imposed boundaries" between the Fellows so they could operate as a "single intelligence for the good of their communities."

It was a year or so after my meeting with Bohm that the Harvard biologist, E. O. Wilson, popularized the *biophilia hypothesis* that our evolutionary history has blessed us with an innate affinity for nature. The appeal of the natural is reflected in where we most want to live. Many studies have shown that even a limited exposure to nature, like a chance to look at the natural world through a window, is good for your health. Hospitalized patients heal more quickly when there is a window to the outside world, and prisoners get sick less often. Virtually all indigenous cultures have regarded nature as the ultimate teacher, as have all great poets, painters, and scientists, such as Newton and Einstein.

These powerful effects of nature were well known to me, but I didn't understand the cause until years later when I met Ian Player, a leader of nature retreats in the African wilderness. Founder of the Wilderness Leadership School in South Africa, Dr. Player is often referred to as "the man who saved the white rhino."

Ian and I spent a weekend together in 2002 at the conference in Putten where I had met the Unilever chairman, Antony Burgmans. The following week, Ian and I met in London where I absorbed all I could of his penetrating wisdom. Ian explained that thousands of years of human evolution are imprinted in our psyche. Spending time alone in nature is at the core of our genetic coding. We are virtually identical to the people who lived at the end of the Ice Age and who possessed capacities that lie dormant in us today, including a heightened sense of awareness and knowing beyond the limited self. I believe it was the mythologist Joseph Campbell who talked about feeling the rhythms of life in the wilds of nature – "the rhythm of our own heartbeat is the rhythm of the universe and when we are in accord with this universal rhythm, we feel most alive." Ian said that when we are in solitude in nature, we enter a world of long-past experiences and become free again – our "secret birthright."

Ian's view of the generative power of nature has been confirmed by my direct experience of over thirty years, especially my three extraordinary experiences of communication with animals – the ermine in the Tetons described in *Synchronicity*, the whales in Baja, and the mountain lion in Montana. Ian's view has also been confirmed by virtually every remarkable person I've interviewed about the source of the entrepreneurial impulse, including John Milton, Brian Arthur, David Bohm, and the scientists at Pari, Princeton, and HeartMath. The consistent experiences of the participants in Innovation Labs over the years underscore his views as well.

The wilderness passage provides a liminal experience, the root from which our highest characteristics and experiences can grow. In the wilderness, self-realization is born, and over time, it can mature into a distinctive kind of awareness, which has been described in the ancient texts for thousands of years. Descriptions of this kind of awareness are found among the traditional beliefs of people in every region of the world, and in its fully developed form, it has its place among every one of the world's major religions. Such a passage for a management team in an Innovation Lab acts to dissolve the team's self-imposed boundaries, enabling it to operate as a single intelligence to resolve the issue at hand.

>-+-+>-·O-·<+-+-<

Over the years, we've learned that taking groups or teams to sacred sites enhances their capacity to gain access to new knowledge. All cultures have celebrated particular places as powerful. The Japanese word *ba*, "place," is used to refer not only to a physical place, but also to an existential place that arises from the interaction and patterns of relationships that evolve among participants in any undertaking of mutual importance. Used in this sense, *ba* transcends time and space.

The subject of such "conditioned space" was at the heart of the Field Paper as well as the salon we held in Boston with Nonaka. *Ba* is the field Bohm described in which true dialogue occurs. Bohm told me that such positive fields can be set by our "intention and way of being." Bob and Brenda told me that it was accepted in their scientific circles that space can be conditioned this way.

I told them of Professor Tiller's conversations with me about sacred sites and "conditioned space." Tiller's studies show that by entering a deep meditative state and then sending or "imprinting" intentions onto RNGs shielded from electromagnetic and human influences, these effects are maintained and even transferred to the space around them. Tiller says that sacred sites, like churches and special holy places, are "conditioned" spaces and retain a certain quality about them that can be measured with simple pH or temperature meters. "Intentions, previously . . . erratic and feeble, now become more constant, more direct, and more ordered." Jahn and Dunne's work confirmed that such conditioned spaces have "more structure, a higher level of order."

35. THE POWER OF LOVE

SOMEDAY, AFTER MASTERING THE WINDS, THE WAVES, THE TIDES, AND GRAVITY,
WE SHALL HARNESS FOR GOD THE ENERGIES OF LOVE AND THEN, FOR A SECOND
TIME IN THE HISTORY OF THE WORLD, MAN WILL HAVE DISCOVERED FIRE.
– Pierre Teilhard de Chardin

Bob and Brenda were crystal clear with me: an essential element
of enhanced access to what we have been calling "the Source" is an
unambiguous commitment in an energy field of service, self-sacrifice, and
love. "Selfless investment of self can affect physical reality," they said.
They have been drawn to this conclusion, they said, not only by their
personal persuasion created over years of developmental practice, but by
the "tangible, objective results encountered on a daily basis over years of
rigorous laboratory experimentation." They also told me that these results
were consistent with the spiritual traditions described in ancient texts
over millennia.

This conclusion – that selfless investment of self can affect physical
reality – was expressed to me during the entire course of my search
for understanding, beginning with Bohm in London and ending with
virtually every scientist at Pari. It is inherent in Bohm's maxim that
"a change of meaning is a change of being." And Lee Nichol's closing
remarks that day in Pari were infused with the point that true Bohmian
Dialogue embraces "the deepest promptings of our humanity."

I was particularly drawn to Jahn's reference to a statement by Prince
Louis de Broglie, whom Jahn described as "one of the patriarchs of
modern physics." It is highly relevant to the role that deep caring plays in
connecting our thoughts and action:

If we wish to give philosophic expression to the profound
connection between thought and action in all fields of human
endeavor, particularly in science, we shall undoubtedly have to
see its sources in the unfathomable depths of the human soul.
Perhaps philosophers might call it "love" in a very general sense
– that force which directs all our actions, which is the source
of all our delights and all our pursuits. Indissolubly linked with
thought and with action, love is their common mainspring and,
hence, their common bond. The engineers of the future have
an essential part to play in cementing this bond.

Bill O'Brien, one of the cofounders of Generon, was the CEO of
Hanover Insurance Company in the 1970s. Bill was a Stage IV leader,
guiding Hanover to become one of the earliest Stage IV organizations.
He was a lifelong student of the philosopher Pierre Teilhard de Chardin,
whose strong orientation was toward oneness and the interconnectedness
of all life. Bill and I had long talks about the new developments in
contemporary psychology, physics, and ecology and their remarkable
convergence with the major insights of Taoism and Teilhard's thought.
Bill often pointed to Teilhard's words: "Someday, after mastering the
winds, the waves, the tides, and gravity, we shall harness for God the
energies of love and then, for a second time in the history of the world,
man will have discovered fire."

In light of my own experience and those of the many teachers,
colleagues, and scientists I had encountered, I felt able to form the
concluding principle:

4. **Humans can learn to draw from the infinite potential of the
    Source by choosing to follow a disciplined path toward self-
    realization and love, the most powerful energy in the universe.**
    The path may include teachings from ancient traditions
    developed over thousands of years, contemplative practices, and
    direct exposure to the generative process of nature.

36. A DISCIPLINED PATH

SOURCE CAN BECOME ACTIVE IN YOUR LIFE, AND YOU CAN
PARTICIPATE WITH SOURCE IF YOU ARE WILLING TO DO THE
WORK TO BECOME ADEQUATE TO DO SO.
  – John Milton

Bohm saw the body as "the individual gateway to a remarkable wealth of unexpected information" – *if* "consistent and deep" personal work was done. This fact of life has been known since antiquity and constitutes one of the features essential to enable enhanced communication with the Source that I talked about with Jahn and Dunne. They specifically mentioned meditation, qigong, and yoga as practices that provide heightened access to the Source. And of course these same principles are at the very heart of John Milton's awareness training and the observations of the HeartMath research team as they studied successful entrepreneurs. The years Brian spent in Hong Kong with his Taoist teacher focused on such disciplines. Michael Polanyi wrote extensively about the "ancient systems of contemplation" designed to "release us not only from the intellectual framework of perception but from our very existence as individual transmigrating beings," enabling discovery and innovation.

The most recent scientific studies have shown that deliberate practices such as these, performed over time, can produce changes in the brain and central nervous system, making possible new levels of awareness. It's not so important whether the contemplative practice is meditation, qigong, aikido, tai chi, or any number of other disciplines found throughout the world. What's important is the commitment to follow a disciplined path toward self-realization.

But if I'm a complete novice, how do I begin?

The first thing to note is that this question – "How do I begin?" – occurs in two sets of circumstances, individual and collective. In the Waco crisis or the Innovation Labs, the question is, "How do we *collectively* gain access to the Source?" – a question I'll discuss later.

But for *individual* access to the Source, there are many different types of experiences. One involves a sudden illumination – for example, when I saw the whales in Baja, I fell to my knees sobbing, knowing my life would never be the same again. Out of this experience rose the deep commitment to create the Global Leadership Initiative. Another kind of experience would be illumination that arises when someone (or a group) has been trying, over time, to resolve a tough issue (like Brian on his theory of increasing returns, or Jonas Salk discovering the polio vaccine). Then there is an important knowing that suddenly occurs from Source – for example, the knowing that I had to do whatever it took to get in touch with Brian Arthur, or the experience of my friend Kees van der Graaf, a member of the Board of Directors of Unilever and responsible for Unilever's European business. Kees and his management team had been struggling to discover a robust strategy to deal with a significantly complex and volatile business environment, but had found no satisfactory solution to the challenges they faced. In the middle of a solo wilderness experience in Montana, it suddenly occurred to Kees how to proceed. He pulled out his little notepad from his shirt pocket and began to write feverishly for over an hour, filling his notebook. He reported in the circle that as a result of that breakthrough, "I now know what to do." There was not a hint of uncertainty in his voice.

Then there is what I call "living and working from Source." Although this is a less dramatic, more everyday experience of decision-making and creative problem-solving, it is, in many ways, just as important as those more dramatic revelations. One example of "living and working from Source" is what occurred for me back in 2005 when I was living in the North Shore of Boston. For several years, I had been considering whether to move to Stowe, Vermont, but in listing out the pros and cons, things became too complicated. There were just too many intangibles. So I had put the idea aside and forgotten about it.

Then early one morning, when I was doing qigong in the backyard of my home, suddenly there flashed before me the idea: "Sell the home and move to Stowe." When I finished the qigong session, I went inside and reflected for just a moment. Then without any hesitation, I picked up the telephone and called my friend, the realtor who had sold my current home to me seven years previously. "Ron, I've decided to sell this home. Please get an appraisal and let's get it on the market." Again, there was not a hint of uncertainty in my voice, in my heart. There was no handwringing. The decision was final. It turns out that this was one of the better decisions of my life.

Incidentally, Ron called me back the next morning with the ballpark sales figure. We put the house on the market using this number, and later that same day, Ron called me back. "You won't believe this, but I have a professor from the West Coast who is extremely interested. Can he and his wife come by this afternoon?" We signed the contract of sale for the asking price the following morning, and I was moving one month later.

>—I—◆>—O—◆—I—<

There are three features to keep in mind as one learns to live and work from the Source:

1. THE SHIFT FROM RESIGNATION TO POSSIBILITY

Seeing the world as open and full of possibility is the fundamental shift of mind that opens the door to connecting to the Source. Each of us has a capacity for awe, wonder, and reverence. The human species has an inbuilt passion to serve life, to learn, to know, and to experience the thrill of discovery. At the heart of the path Polanyi describes there is the *passionate pursuit of hidden meaning* – the act of creating something of significance that has never existed before. Each of us can choose to let go of the obstacles that impede our development and to release the possibilities that lie latent within each of us.

2. THE INNER WORK

Contemplative Practices: By far, the most accessible and conventional contemplative practice is that of meditation. There are two levels of experiencing the practice of meditation. The first is the aspect of *concentration*, which brings calmness and stability of mind to the practitioner. Concentration leads to the second level, *mindfulness*, which allows the practitioner to see greater relationships among things and gives him access to "a far greater range of information, a truly generative place." Bringing such awareness into one's life influences everything, because it influences the very next moment. "Such awareness is generative – it creates new possibilities." This is the level Lee Nichol spoke of at Pari when he said something beyond thought comes into operation – a conscious awareness that is *primary* and that is genuinely a new order of insight.

Energy Practice: An important complement to the practice of meditation is energy practice – the cultivation of universal energy. There are a number of methods for cultivating universal energy including qigong, tai chi, and Aikido. By far the most popular in the East is qigong. Qi (pronounced "chee") is the Chinese word for "life energy." According to Chinese medicine, qi is the animating power that flows through all living things. Qigong is an ancient practice that includes movement, breathing techniques, stillness, and meditation. Through the practice, qi is accumulated and stored in the body. Students generally practice twenty to forty minutes per day, preferably in the morning in nature. It has become accepted today in some business circles that qigong can help participants stay centered and make wise decisions in the face of challenging circumstances, particularly when the stakes are high.

Many of the remarkable people I've met have mentioned energy practices as a way to cleanse their perceptions – and this cleansing helps enable connection to the Source. I highly recommend two resources for beginners in this practice: John P. Milton's *Qigong for Long Life* and Kenneth S. Cohen's *The Way of Qigong, the Art and Science of Chinese Energy Healing*. Cohen observes that "qigong strengthens the intuition.

Synchronicity becomes almost commonplace as you find yourself more often in the right place at the right time."

Spending Time in Nature: Spending quiet time in a natural setting is an important portal to personal development and enables access to the Source. Qigong practice early in the morning in one's backyard or in a park is a perfect avenue to gaining consistent access to the Source. Walks in solitude in nature – for example, in a park or arboretum early in the morning – is an ideal practice. When possible, I return to familiar places in nature where I have previously been practicing. It's the same principle one would follow in establishing a strong relationship in the world of humans.

A wilderness passage every twelve to eighteen months is a powerful way to profoundly deepen the cultivation of universal energy and connection with the Source.

And when one confronts a decision that is important to one's life and less susceptible to resolution by scientific decision theory – decisions like "Should I marry this person?" or "Should I follow this career?" or "Should I sell my company?" or "When should we go public?" – it helps to follow Brian Arthur's advice and go to that deeper place, doing the work necessary to notice the cues and evidence emerging from the environment. Then let it go. Take a long walk in the woods alone and go to that "deeper region of consciousness." Then follow your inner knowing.

3. THE COURAGE TO ACT IN AN INSTANT

It takes courage to listen to your inner knowing – to the Source. But once you hear that knowing, making a decision becomes fairly easy. You don't think or strategize. You just know. It's a kind of battle-hardened confidence that emerges from within. There is a fearlessness – a risk-it-all intention, uncommon in our normal way of operating, that emerges in these moments. And inwardly, we *know* that the risk is acceptable.

Take, for example, when I was in the back of the auditorium at the Shell Learning Center outside of Houston. When I heard Glen Tilton's words, it was as if a power switch had been turned on. An extraordinary energy was released. As David Peat put it, "The creative energy that is let loose at this moment can be compared to that released in a nuclear reaction, when the internal structure of the nucleus is re-arranged. Energy is directed to new possibilities. The future and its endless possibilities become open to creative change."

After Tilton concluded his remarks, I ran to set up the lunch with Gary Jusela and poured my heart out to him and to Jim Morgan the following morning. There was no planning or strategizing about how to frame my proposal. It just flowed out of me, without conscious thought or control. These are the characteristics – the excitement, the clarity, the anticipation, and absolute certainty – that often accompany the breakthrough moment.

>─I─◆>─O─<◆─I─<

Over time, I've learned an important life lesson: when you're operating from Source, there is no doubt. You know what to do, and you just do it. There's a rightness to it.

37. DEVELOPING STAGE IV
LEADERSHIP

KNOWLEDGE IS A FUNCTION OF BEING.
– Aldous Huxley

I've thought about how to describe the values and qualities of character that form the foundation of Stage IV Leadership and decided that the best way to do this was to tell about a man I had the privilege to work with who was a clear exemplar of that stage: Admiral James Bond Stockdale. Jim Stockdale's story also reflects the vital nature of the quality of preparation that is necessary to make one adequate to live in and operate from the Source.

When I met Admiral Stockdale in 1980, he was recently retired from serving as president of the Naval War College and was teaching philosophy at Stanford University. I invited him to join the Board of Trustees of the American Leadership Forum, where he helped design the curriculum and taught the pilot course, serving with us for almost nine years.

Learning from Stockdale during many intimate conversations was a great gift. His experiences as a prisoner of war are highly relevant to my search for an understanding of the Source, particularly in relation to the essential personal characteristics that allow one to experience self-realization through a traumatic experience.

Developing this kind of character is a theme of the *perennial philosophy* – a phrase defined by the philosopher Aldous Huxley as referring to "the metaphysic that recognizes a divine Reality substantial in the world of things and lives and minds; the psychology that finds in the Soul something similar to, or even identical with, divine Reality; the ethic that places man's final end in the knowledge of the immanent and transcendent Ground of all being – the thing immemorial and universal." Huxley said that "Rudiments of the Perennial Philosophy may be found among the traditional lore of primitive peoples in every region of the world, and in its fully developed forms it has a place in every one of the higher religions. A version of this Highest Common Factor in all preceding and subsequent theologies was first committed to writing more than twenty-five centuries ago, and since that time the inexhaustible theme has been treated again and again, from the standpoint of every religious tradition and in all the principal languages of Asia and Europe."

Referring to the essential prerequisites to gaining access to primary knowing, or as he put it, "immediate apprehension and intuitive power," Huxley wrote:

> Knowledge is a function of being. When there is a change in the being of the Knower, there is a corresponding change in the nature and amount of knowing . . . what we know depends on what, as moral beings, we choose to make ourselves. "Practice" in the words of William James, "may change our theoretical horizon, and this in a twofold way: it may lead into new worlds and secure new powers. Knowledge we could never attain, remaining what we are, may be attainable in consequence of higher powers and a higher life which we may morally achieve." . . . (T)he nature of this one Reality is such that it cannot be directly and immediately apprehended except by those who have chosen to fulfill certain conditions, making themselves loving, pure in heart, and poor in Spirit. . . . In the ordinary circumstances of average sensual life, those potentialities of the mind remain latent and un-manifested. If we would realize them, we must fulfill certain conditions and obey certain rules, which experience has shown empirically to be valid.

In September 1965, then Wing Commander Airborne Stockdale was shot down on a combat mission over North Vietnam, severely breaking his leg during ejection. Stockdale was captured and taken to prison in Central Hanoi. He spent the next seven-and-a-half-years there, four of them in solitary confinement. As the senior officer among the prisoners, he was responsible for defining rules of conduct and maintaining morale. Because of his rank, he was considered to be a prime political asset.

Because his captors believed that sooner or later his will would be broken and that he could then be used for propaganda purposes, they subjected him to the most brutal torture, intimidation, and isolation. But he responded with intelligence, courage, and exceptional creativity. Soon after his release in the spring of 1973, he was awarded the Congressional Medal of Honor, America's highest commendation for bravery, for risking his life to protect his fellow prisoners.

Stockdale told me, reluctantly, some of what he endured over those seven-and-a-half years. He was in solitary confinement in a tiny, dark, filthy, windowless "concrete box." Regularly, he was subjected to "being beat to a bloody pulp." He was placed in "torture cuffs" for weeks at a time; locked in a stock for weeks on end; bound in ropes by "tourniquet-wielding torture specialists who could make you scream like a baby."

"They can make you tell them almost anything they know you know," he said. "The trick is, year in and year out, never to level with them, never let them really know what you know." His mother was a drama coach and had taught him acting as a young child. He used what he learned to keep his captors off balance. In the face of all of this, he devised a tap-code system and taught it to his fellow prisoners so they could communicate even while in solitary.

Further, over the course of the second year in prison, Stockdale corresponded with the Office of Naval Intelligence through letters to and from his wife, Sybil, using his urine and a special invisible carbon paper that was embedded between a photograph Sybil sent him and its backing. Incredibly, he transmitted to Naval Intelligence the names of the forty or so American prisoners he could positively identify through his tap-code system. He also sent descriptions and statistics about the torture that was taking place in his prison. Stockdale said his purpose while living in that prison was twofold: "the practical problem of daily survival" and "to return home with honor."

I talked with Jim Stockdale for hours about his ordeal and how he was able not just to survive but to perform at such an exceptional level over a sustained period of time. His response: self-preparation – he systematically prepared himself both before and during the ordeal.

Before his imprisonment, he had developed a structured set of values that supported a basic principle of self-reliance and self-respect. He said this was fundamental to his performance. He pointed to a gift a professor of philosophy had given to him during the last day of his postgraduate study at Stanford. It was a copy of *The Enchiridion* by Epictetus. Epictetus was the son of a Roman slave, and this particular book was what might be considered a manual for the combat officer of that time. Stockdale read this book that evening and was puzzled. "Why had the professor chosen this reading as a parting gift? I was an organizer of men and a fighter pilot, concerned with the technology of the age. How could the foundations of the Aurelian Stoical School apply to my daily life? My questions were answered in Vietnam," he said. "When I ejected from that airplane in 1965, I left the world of technology and entered the world of Epictetus."

Stockdale reduced the elements of his self-preparation to these four:

1. **Integrity – Dedication to the Truth**
   "Above all else, keep your conscience clean. If you don't lose your integrity, you can't be had and you can't be hurt. . . . Glib, cerebral and detached people can get by in positions of authority until the pressure is on. But when the crunch develops, people cling to those they know they can trust – those who are not detached, but involved – and those who have consciences. . . ."

2. **Assumption of Responsibility and Discharge of One's Obligation and Duty**
   "Duty can be understood without reference to external law or to compulsion, divine or human. We share this understanding whenever – having made a promise, taken an oath, contracted a debt of duty – we feel an obligation to discharge it, even if no superior commands the act. Duty in this perspective has absolute character. Duty is its own justification. It does not have to be propped up by anything outside itself, particularly in the line of reward or punishment. This was the teaching of Socrates who urged men should obey the law, pay their debts, discharge their obligations, not to avoid the pain of censure or punishment, but simply because they ought to."

3. **Self-Discipline and the Delay of Gratification**
   A principle Stockdale lived by before, during, and after his prison ordeal was the following: "Self-discipline is vital to self-respect;

self-indulgence is fatal." Stockdale said that undertaking daily practices is essential to mental and spiritual health. In prison, he and his fellow prisoners found they had to build a daily ritual into their lives "to avoid becoming an animal." For almost all of them, he said, their daily practices were built around prayer, meditation, exercise, and clandestine communication. "I would do four-hundred pushups a day, even when I had leg irons on, and would feel guilty when I failed to do them." He said, "The prayers I said were prayers of quality with ideas of substance."

4. **Love and Community**

Stockdale was utterly clear about the power of love, comradeship, and community. When he was asked, "What kept you going? What was your highest value?" his answer always was, "The man next door." He had an abiding belief that there was enormous power in comradeship, bonds of mutual trust, and love for one another. "This love, this unity, this mutual trust and confidence is a source of power as old as man, one we forget in times of freedom, of affluence, of fearful pessimism," he said. "In prison, our world literally became our band of brothers; our personal pride and our reputation among our peers was our total life investment."

Stockdale wrote that, for him, Principle One is that you are your brothers' keeper:

> In an environment in which people are trying to manipulate others – be it prison, a rigid hierarchical organization, or a bloated bureaucracy – there is always the temptation to better your own position by thinking only about yourself. Yet, sooner or later, it becomes clear that the greater good for you and your fellow inmates, the key to happiness, self-respect and survival, lies in submerging your individual instincts for self-preservation to the greater common denominator of universal solidarity.
>
> The opportunist may make significant short-term gains by walking over his fellow workers, by taking credit for their good work, or by selfish theatrics. But each time he loses faith with his peers, he forfeits some of his self-respect.

Stockdale was a supremely private man and seldom chose to talk of his faith or the Divine. However, he said that during his confinement, at the moment of maximum danger to his life, suddenly the face of Christ "popped out of nowhere" in front of him – the same face, he said, he saw every Sunday on the big stained-glass window of the U.S. Naval Academy chapel just behind the altar. "He's looking right into me, just like he used to when I was a plebe sitting before Him at mandatory chapel every Sunday, praying that I could make it at Annapolis." At the very same moment of the vision, he was able to make split-second decisions that enabled him to avoid detection of his secret messages by two guards who had just entered his cell.

Connection with the Source comes in many different forms. It seems to me that Stockdale's religious faith allowed him to "see" that connection at a moment of extreme crisis in the form of an image that he had initially observed behind the altar of the Naval Academy. In that way, his discipline, his sense of duty, and his faith merged in that instant of connection, allowing him the kind of "knowing" that led him to make a life-saving decision in an instant.

38. SCAFFOLDING STAGE IV
ORGANIZATIONS

*AS THE ORGANIZATION ADVANCES AND GROWS, CERTAIN CORE PRACTICES BEGIN
TO DEFINE THE CULTURE OF THE ENTERPRISE, BECOMING ITS "WAY OF BEING."*

Our institutions are facing profound change and rising complexity,
accelerating at a scale, intensity, and speed never experienced before.
As the economic foundations of our world are transformed from more
stable to dynamic patterns, the nature of leadership must change as well.
To succeed in this new environment, institutional leadership must pay
attention to the tacit Source of knowledge, the deep Source from which
profound innovation occurs.

Organizations led by people with this quality of knowing, from line
leaders to the very top, will flourish in the decades to come. Because
of their success, they will become "living examples" of what is possible
in the face of accelerating complexity and high turbulence. These
Stage IV organizations will play a leading role in establishing a more
comprehensive worldview, a belief system adequate for civilization to rise
above the challenges of our time.

Those organizations advancing to Stage IV must develop core
practices that inspire innovation and action and enable advanced
decision-making, breakthrough strategy formation, operational excellence,
and profound innovation. To develop such practices and use them
successfully requires an organization to grow and develop through stages,
just as humans do. Recall Lievegoed's insight that the phases and the
development of the human being are themselves an archetype for the
development of organizations.

Organizations can be systematically developed through stages of maturity. The decision by the chief executive and the top management team to commit to Stage IV renewal is not dissimilar from the decision Polanyi describes in his structure of knowledge creation – the voyage of discovery the innovator in any field travels in the process of advancement of knowledge. It is a sacred undertaking on the part of the top team, driven by a sense of responsibility for advancing the growth of the organization's capacity to flourish in the face of rising complexity and rapid change. This is a commitment to pursue a path of maturation that departs in a deep sense from what went before.

⊱┈◈┈○┈◈┈⊰

Developing a whole organization to a Stage IV level requires a number of actions:

- Focusing on the growth of the senior team and a critical mass of change leaders to demonstrate commitment and trigger multiplier effects.

- Refining and reaffirming the organization's guiding ideas and basic assumptions (similar to those reflected in the Four Principles and the three features outlined in Chapter 36).

- Focusing on the critical three-to-five shifts needed to unlock the potential of the organization. Focusing first on a critical few elements gives coherence to the undertaking.

- Magnifying the positive attitudes, behaviors, and practices that already exist and facilitating an expanded view of individual and organizational potential to do more of those. Later-stage organizations have a greater capacity to self-correct and learn from their mistakes than do those in earlier stages of development.

- Cascading opportunities for personal growth and development throughout the organization.

The most critical principle for success is one less well known: *scaffolding* the organization's developmental growth. The term "scaffolding" is associated with a Russian psychologist, Lev Vygotsky, who used it to refer to structuring participation in learning encounters in order to foster a child's emerging growth and development to reach his or her fullest potential as a mature human being. In organizations, scaffolding is the practice of matching employee development with operational work, providing a daily opportunity for business transactions to be used as a learning vehicle. Each operation and each transaction is performed with the consciousness and awareness accompanying the more comprehensive worldview embraced by the Four Principles.

Scaffolding is the infrastructure the organization establishes to ensure that each person is dedicated to teaching others what he or she has learned while at the same time learning something new from others. This is the method by which Stage IV practices become embedded in the fabric of the day-to-day life of the enterprise.

A changing quality of support takes place over time. A more skilled partner adjusts the assistance he or she provides to fit the other's level of development and current level of performance. More support is offered when a task is new and less when the other's development and competence increases, thereby encouraging the other's autonomy and independent mastery.

The chief executive and the senior team develop the enterprise into a teaching and learning community, a system that matures everyone through daily work. Work becomes a pedagogy – the science of teaching. Kaz is a pioneer of this practice and calls this the "Nothing Extra" approach to developing a Stage IV organization.

>─┼─◆>─○─◆─┼─<

As the organization advances and grows, certain core practices begin to define the culture of the enterprise, becoming its "way of being." Every organization has its own culture – its pattern of shared basic assumptions, guiding ideas, operating principles, and core practices. When appropriately introduced and applied throughout the organization, these core elements enable the organization to perform at exceptional levels.

The seven core practices of the new U-process, which we call *Generative Discovery*, when performed with the worldview embraced by the Four Principles, are paramount:

1. **Preparation:** Undertaking a disciplined path of inner self-management.

2. **Igniting Passion:** Making a firm commitment to pursue the inquiry, being guided by the intensely personal foreknowledge that the solution being sought exists as a hidden possibility.

3. **Observing and Immersing:** Seeing reality with fresh eyes, suspending judgment and immersion in the existing data.

4. **Letting Go:** Releasing currently held mental models, mindsets, and worldviews; beginning a period of incubation.

5. **Indwelling and Illumination:** Living in the undertaking, surrendering oneself to the work, absorbed in the experience; retreating, using the generative processes of nature as a portal to learning and new knowledge; and receiving illumination – the perception of a new reality, discovering the hidden solution.

6. **Crystallizing and Prototyping:** Moving through a period of crystallization and prototyping, making manifest what was discovered.

7. **Testing and Verifying:** Transforming the new knowledge into usable products, decisions, or strategies.

These seven practices embody a single experience – that of actualizing potentials lying dormant in the universe and discovering orders of reality beyond our rational understanding and cocreating with that which is ready to emerge. This process of Generative Discovery – the advanced version of the U-process – embraces the views that Bohm, Brian Arthur, the scientists at Pari and Princeton, and Polanyi expressed and is key to the advancement of an organization to Stage IV as well as to the creation of knowledge that enables the enterprise to perform at exceptional levels.

There is a critical distinction between the process of Generative Discovery and that which was used in the less successful Demonstration Project (Partnership for Child Nutrition). The practitioners of the original U-process emphasized intelligence and years of experience in organizational development and facilitation; but the essence of

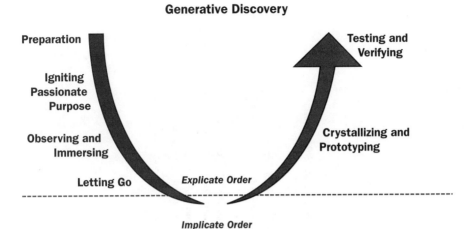

Generative Discovery

Preparation

Testing and Verifying

Igniting Passionate Purpose

Observing and Immersing

Crystallizing and Prototyping

Letting Go

Explicate Order

Implicate Order

Indwelling and Illumination

the process of Generative Discovery is (1) being open to alternative worldviews; (2) operating from the stance of human possibility; and (3) tapping into the generative orders of the universe, the field of active information – the Source.

The seven practices can also be used as an Innovation Lab in discrete projects, such as we did with the Alliance and in the Demonstration Projects. In these instances, the selection of the Lab team is vital. The team must be a "microcosm," representative of the organization or divisions affected. The importance of this was stressed in Pari by Henri Bortoft, when he spoke of "having the whole system in the room" and in the final conversation about the critical role that the team's purpose and values play in the successful outcome of the Innovation Lab.

The whole process of Generative Discovery is infused with meaning. Truth and love are at its core. The collective "intention and way of being" on the part of the Lab team – the respect and deep caring for the whole system under investigation – enables the collapse of boundaries Bohm spoke of and allows the team to operate as a single intelligence for the good of the enterprise. At this moment of oneness, the participants act out of the unfolding generative order, the unbroken wholeness from which seemingly discrete discoveries take place. It is at this moment that

Innovation Lab
One Process — Eight Elements

Implementation of Solutions

Presentation of Results: From microcosm prototypes to Venture Committee.

Learning by Doing: Prototype strategic microcosms.

Common Commitment: Present and choose prototyping initiatives.

Explicate Order

Implicate Order

Innovation Retreat

Co-initiation: Identify opportunities, stakeholders, core players; conduct deep dialogue interviews.

Foundation Workshops: Create shared understanding of purpose, process, roles, and responsibilities.

Learning Journeys: Arrange for total immersion in relevant contexts.

striking new realities are enacted for the benefit of the whole enterprise and the whole system.

The key to the process is that it is designed to bring forth the emerging reality *as it desires*. To act on behalf of the future in this way requires a deep sense of responsibility and selflessness. I think that's one reason Polanyi used the term *fiduciary act* for this kind of undertaking. The term *fiduciary* is deeply meaningful to me because it's a legal term that's used when you're talked about a trustee's responsibility or the responsibility of a lawyer when acting for a client. My father, also a lawyer, infused his whole life with this kind of responsibility and ethic of selfless service, and he raised me to aspire to this credo. When I took the professional oath in becoming a lawyer, I promised to act for my client, taking my own personal interests completely out of the picture.

So when I came across Polanyi's insistence that originality is guided by a sense of responsibility for advancing the growth of truth "in men's minds," I understood, deep in my heart, what he meant by saying of originality that "its freedom lies in this perfect service."

39. STAGE IV ENTERPRISES: TWO STORIES

I KNEW IT WAS GOING TO WORK OUT, SOMEHOW, SOME WAY.
WE JUST "LAID A PATH AS WE WALKED IT."
– Gary Wilson

A detailed explanation of the transformation of a company from an earlier stage to a Stage IV enterprise is beyond the scope of this book. But some of the potential power and creativity that access to the Source offers to companies can be seen through stories. Here are two examples.

In the first story, a man connects to the Source through a near-death experience – with significant results not only for his own personal life but also for his work in the world and for the enterprise he led. The second is of a man I briefly introduced in the early pages of this book – Gary Wilson – who co-led a Los Angeles refinery during 1999–2002 as it went from "worst to first" among the eighteen refineries in the Alliance.

DAVID MARSING'S FAB 11

Sometimes revelation comes after a serious personal crisis, such as a heart attack. Paraphrasing the poet William Blake, the doors of perception are cleansed and things appear as they really are. We have all heard of such experiences. But this one is special to me because David Marsing is a close friend of mine.

During the time David was a senior officer at Intel, he suffered a near-fatal heart attack. He traces the origin of his capacity to lead to the clarity and sense of purpose that arose from that heart attack. This is the story he told for us in a number of workshops:

I died, clinically, in the emergency room. Fortunately, they
brought me back. As I lay on the gurney, I knew exactly why
I was there: I'd had the heart attack because of the way I was
living. I always knew that Intel was a high-stress environment,
but I'd thought of myself as somehow above it. I'd been an
athlete. I'd worked there for many years. I was tough. But I was
also blind. I was blind to what the environment I'd helped to
create did to people, including me. As I lay there, I saw all of
this very clearly. I also knew that climbing the ladder at Intel
was really not very important to me.

In the hospital and during the months afterward, I
discovered that my true purpose was to help people realize
that they have more potential than they ever imagined they
had. I made a conscious choice to go back into that stressful
environment, but to do it with a very different perspective
and with much more concentration on my meditative and
spiritual processes. I wanted to create environments for
people that would help them see their true, full potential. I
also wanted to protect people from the typical responses that
large organizations generate when they're under stress. These
responses can be very unhealthy, as I'd discovered first hand.

David did many things differently when he returned to work. One was
to introduce reflective or contemplative practices at alternating weekly
staff meetings. He said, "At first people weren't sure if I was serious. Many
doubted that it would last. But over time they found these very helpful in
slowing down, being much more aware of their environment and opening
up."

Eventually, these new practices and David's new outlook led to
one of Intel's biggest successes. David was general manager during the
construction and "ramp-up" of Fab 11, Intel's biggest semiconductor
fabrication facility and at the time the largest "fab" of its kind in the
world. Fab 11 went from start-up to full-volume production in record
time, allowing Intel to recoup its $2.5-billion investment not in several
years, as expected, but in just five short months.

>─┼─◆>─O─<◆─┼─◄

A few years ago, I was delivering a workshop in the Netherlands.
One of the participants was a cardiologist who gave me an essay in
manuscript form that described the near-death experience as a portal to
the intelligence of the Source, precisely as Jahn and Dunne had described.

It was called "Near-Death Experience (NDE), Consciousness and the Brain" and had been written by the cardiologist's colleague, Pim van Lommel, a respected Dutch cardiologist practicing at Rijnstate Hospital in Arnhem, the Netherlands. Van Lommel concluded that the NDE is a "transformation, causing profound changes of life, insight, and loss of the fear of death."

The source of this "profound transformation," he said, is an interconnectedness with informational fields of consciousness called the zero-point field. "This extended or enhanced consciousness is based on indestructible and constantly evolving fields of information where all knowledge, wisdom, and unconditional Love are present and available, and these fields of consciousness are stored in a dimension without our concept of time and space, with non-local and universal interconnectedness. One could call this our Higher consciousness, Divine consciousness, or Cosmic consciousness."

During David's college years, he practiced martial arts and wrestling. In both of these pursuits, he attained a high degree of mastery. After his near-fatal heart attack, David made a commitment to daily personal practices, which included meditation, prayer, and qigong. He built a meditation room in the backyard of his home in Santa Fe, New Mexico, and worked regularly with a Taoist master to facilitate his personal development, moral sensitivity, and intuitive awareness. His comprehensive program for personal growth and development was designed to deepen his capacity "to be true to myself and maintain pure intentions" as well as deepen his capacity for "deeper and different ways of knowing. . . . I wanted to integrate and embody the intuitive practices I felt were needed in Intel's highly analytical culture. The traditional teachings suggest that you need to practice something 10,000 times correctly before you 'know' it. At this stage you've mastered it, and don't have to think about the mechanical execution."

When he accepted the assignment to be general manager of the start-up at Fab 11, he committed to himself that he would "create an environment for breakthrough performance at every level – not just in traditional work indicators, but interpersonally, and in terms of the individual integration of work and personal life." Fab 11 was to be the world's largest semiconductor fabrication plant, with 200,000 square feet of "clean room." Three or four times a minute, all the air is flushed out of that room. With all the support and construction, the plant at its peak involved 4,000 people with a $2.2-billion capital investment, meaning that the plant had to produce revenue projected at $1.7-million an hour by the third year.

"With all this at stake," David said, "it's always been a challenge to maintain autonomy. A lot of people at corporate headquarters want to help us make decisions. We had a results-oriented, technology-driven, assertive, risk-oriented corporate culture. Our focus on analytical, rational thinking and decision-making is very strong." David created an understanding with his superiors that allowed him to operate in his new assignment in a "state of negotiated freedom." He lost his fear of failure: "If I couldn't make it work, I figured I could always go be a librarian or a forest ranger."

Contrary to accepted practice at Intel, David spent six months developing the people at Fab 11 *before* construction began. The training included:

- The MIT/OLC Core Course and expanded training in the five learning disciplines;

- Dialogue practices, based on David Bohm's work;

- Work on developing the capacity for good listening, balancing advocacy, and inquiry;

- Human Dynamics training, designed to help people integrate their own learning styles with other personalities on a team; and

- Meditation and other contemplative practices both to manage stress and to develop greater intuitive capacity.

A great deal of emphasis was placed on helping people let go of exclusive reliance on analysis. "In staff meetings, we introduced reflective and contemplative practices designed to help people tap into their innate ability and their true essence. We encouraged people to speak from the heart and learn to look at the factory floor from a sensory perspective. The objective was to help people start to use a different part of their brain. We taught them the positive effect of slower brainwave states as a way to develop an awareness that leads to unique solutions."

One example of the results of this training occurred with a production supervisor who was responsible for an IC chip production line who had named one of her machines "Annie." One day, the supervisor noticed that Annie "felt sick." After a detailed investigation, it was found that the produced IC wafers were close to off-spec. Thanks to her instincts and the quick response of the support teams, tens of millions of dollars worth of product was saved. Collective intelligence develops when people can rely on their instincts and a different way of knowing.

"In the end, we broke all records at Intel for the ramp-up of Fab 11, achieving full-scale operation nine to twelve months faster than the most aggressive estimate. This saved the company over $2.5 billion in cost, not to mention the market benefits of having the new chips we were making available that much sooner. This was an experience of monumental proportions for me – a personal journey of learning and profound personal development. Without the continuous guidance enabled by my personal practices, I would never have been able to help create the culture shift that was core to this result."

GARY WILSON AND THE LOS ANGELES REFINERY

Gary Wilson was the deputy manager of the Los Angeles Refinery Corporation (LARC), one of eighteen in the Alliance, and one of the largest downstream operations in the world (refinery, distribution, and marketing). Gary and the general manager of LARC, Jim Nichols, had been appointed to their positions soon after the Alliance was formed in early 1998. I had known Jim for years because of the work Kaz and I had done with him during the Shell Oil Company transformation. That transformation had begun in the early 1990s and was the subject of the 1998 Field Paper that Kaz, Peter, and I had written. Gary had worked for Texaco most of his working life, rising through the ranks quickly because of his inherent capacity for leadership. In the later years, Gary had developed the capacity for Stage III leadership.

Jim and Gary had inherited a refinery with a workforce of roughly five hundred, which had been ranked by the well-regarded Solomon Survey of operating refineries as among the bottom 25 percent in the world. Together, they decided to begin a systemwide change process with Gary assuming overall responsibility for the transformation.

In June 1998, Gary led the kickoff of what he called the "LARC Change the Business Initiative." The design of the initiative was based on Gary's capacity for Stage III Servant Leadership and on, he told me, what "I knew in my heart – what I knew was possible if the whole workforce environment became one of trust and faith in one another. I knew deep down these people had capacities that were not being used."

A few months later, Gary was invited to join the Innovation Lab design team, consisting of managers from key business units across the Alliance. Later, Gary was chosen as one of about twenty people to participate in the Innovation Lab itself, which I led using the advanced U-process.

The declared purpose of the Lab was written by the Lab team itself and included the following:

- To provide a space for us as Alliance leaders to accelerate our re-invention of Downstream Oil and grow our business and profits.

- To produce practice fields, tools, and coaching to build our individual and collective competencies, energy, and courage.

- To grow our capacity to sense emerging futures and business opportunities.

- To develop our skills to unleash and engage the full creative potential of all Alliance employees.

I spent almost a year working personally with Gary Wilson. It was clear to me from the outset that he had the special qualities possessed by those who could grow and develop into Stage IV leadership. He displayed both humility and self-confidence; his ultimate concern was to serve and develop those in his organization so that they would become healthier, wiser, and more independent. He was entirely open – full of wonder and the desire to learn. He had developed to the point of questioning rigid belief systems. By the time I began working with Gary, he was already in the process of questioning the conventional way of leading and operating a business.

I shared with Gary all I had learned over the past twenty years since I had first met Dr. Bohm. In that process, I gave Gary all the reading material that had been produced during our Alliance research project. We had created a reading list that now appears as a bibliography in the back of *The Red Book*. Those readings included books and essays by Brian Arthur, David Bohm, HeartMath, Larry Dossey, John Kabat-Zinn, and Ikujiro Nonaka. Gary also read *Synchronicity*, the Field Paper, and summaries of the interviews of Brian Arthur and Eleanor Rosch. He spent hours in Santa Fe during the Innovation Lab Wilderness Retreat with Brian Arthur and Professor Michael Ray of Stanford, who is the acknowledged leader in the field of creativity in business and who, for over two decades, taught the essence of what is embraced by the Four Principles.

By the time Gary had emerged from the Lab process, his worldview had matured and his innate values and character had strengthened his courage to take a stand for that which he deeply believed. He began applying his deeper understanding of Stage IV leadership practices during the Lab itself. At the conclusion of the Lab, he began devoting all his energy to the Change the Business Initiative at LARC.

For the kickoff of the process, Gary picked 60 people representing a microcosm of the system, which consisted of some 800 people, including the employees and the outside contractors. He showed them charts of the abysmal refinery performance for the past ten years. He then showed them a blank chart reflecting the next five years. He said, "Let's think together about what's possible. I know we can stretch and reach targets that represent performance at the very top of our industry. Let's create the way forward together. I will give you the freedom to do what's necessary."

The energy in the room was palpable, Gary told me. He was aware of the field effect one person can have in a larger group. At the conclusion of the kickoff meeting, he asked the question, "Who will be willing to make this possibility happen? Who will be part of making this real?" Over 95 percent of the people raised their hands. That's the way the transformation began.

Over the first year, the core change team was expanded from sixty to over twice that many. The essence of the transformation lay in giving each person in the system freedom to bring more of their talents and energies into their work and to operate with a greater sense of ownership and responsibility both for their own work and the work of the system as a whole. Gary said this approach created enthusiasm, satisfaction, and commitment that were infectious and self-reinforcing. The people moved from being spectators to being stewards. Stewardship, Gary said, is a state where people see the whole and their role in it – and they accept responsibility for their role and the whole.

In the old system, each person was required to follow rigid instructions and perform an isolated functional role. Every step of the work process was defined by the manual. If anything went wrong, the automatic response was, "We followed the process in the manual" – thus absolving them of any responsibility. This kind of work, Gary told the craft workers, was suffocating and mind-numbing. What causes the kind of despair and cynicism that existed in the refinery also caused the abysmal performance over the past ten years. Gary told me that high stress and fear were rampant in the system. It was all about "just getting by."

Under the new system, people only had to follow what the refinery called the "Big Rules" provided by management. Gary and his leadership team fulfilled their responsibility by providing guidance and support, monitoring progress all along the way. He and his team made certain that all those in the system felt that they were respected and that their ideas mattered. Work became exciting, enlivening, and even easier. Each person felt ownership: "I own this and am responsible for it and am proud of its performance."

Take for example the pumps in the refinery. Pumps are crucial to the smooth, reliable operation of the refinery – and some of them are quite large. In the process of the transformation, those responsible for the pumps developed a connection to them in almost exactly the same way David Marsing's production supervisor did for "Annie." When anything was amiss, the person responsible for the pump "knew" it before the issue became critical. The pumps were serviced and cared for in a way that had never occurred before. As a sign of their increased sense of ownership of the equipment, some people even began painting "their" pumps their favorite colors. When their family members visited the refinery on an open house tour, they would point out "their" pumps with pride.

This is the way it went throughout the entire refinery. Gary said that he and his management team embraced the principle that performance is dependent on the quality of thought that individual members of the system generate and apply to their work. This higher-order thinking, Gary observed, with resulting high performance is enabled by thinking and acting from principles that illuminate the underlying purpose of the work.

Higher-order thinking was a fundamental feature of Gary's approach. The other fundamental feature related to the belief in "that deeper place of knowing" Gary had learned from Brian Arthur and the whole Lab experience. Gary said that when he had to make a crucial decision, not susceptible to pure analysis, he would follow the U-process and eventually he would, "feel it in my body."

The results are in the numbers. The refinery went "from worst to first" among the eighteen refineries in the Alliance system, and as a direct result of people's performance, not market fluctuations, experienced a $58 million a year earnings improvement. After years of losses, it had become profitable, excelling in all dimensions – improved reliability, safety, and cost. It had the lowest unscheduled downtime among all eighteen refineries.

A few years ago, I asked Gary to reflect on the whole experience. Here is what he told me:

> I look back at this and wonder where I ever got these crazy ideas. They didn't come from a single management book, or work process or anything I had seen work elsewhere. It was all anchored in a sense of purpose that I was brought to this refinery to help 500 people and their families move from feeling like losers to winners, enjoying their life, feeling secure in their future.
>
> There is no doubt in my heart that the whole idea of absorbing and being mindful of what's going on – not just jumping in right away with a decision – is the best way to operate. Just sit back and let it come to you. When the idea hits you, move into action. These past two years, we couldn't make a wrong decision; it was effortless. My premonitions were consistently correct. The U-process is real powerful stuff!

The cost was peanuts compared to the results. What stands out in my learning during the Lab is the Wilderness Retreat. That was the crowning experience because I had the ability to reflect. You have to break away from the day-to-day, immerse yourself in a new way of thinking about yourself. I had a real sense of purpose of why I was in that job. It was a refinery with 500 employees and another 300 contractors, whose lives depended on the plant being successful. I knew I was there to help bring them job security, confidence, and a sense of pride and accomplishment in their lives." Then he paused, and taking a line from *Synchronicity*, concluded: "I knew it was going to work out, somehow, some way. We just 'laid a path as we walked it.'"

For me, that said it all. That's the way it is.

40. THE ADVENT OF STAGE IV
ORGANIZATIONS

STAGE IV ORGANIZATIONS HOLD THE PROMISE OF BEING THE MOST ADAPTIVE INSTITUTIONS HUMANKIND HAS EVER DEVISED.

Developing the capacity to sense and actualize emerging futures constitutes a new form of knowledge creation. Learning to reliably apply the principles and practices expressed in this book, particularly in large organizations and institutions, is a high challenge. That challenge has been met by only a handful of exemplary enterprises. If even a small number of others begin to join them, we could stand on the edge of an epochal transformation. A small number of people in higher states of consciousness can have a disproportionately positive effect on the rest of society, because of the nonlocal effect of human intentions.

Rising Stage IV organizations can become living examples for others to follow. They have the capacity to respond promptly and effectively to accelerating change in the business environment.

Stage IV organizations hold the promise of being the most adaptive institutions humankind has ever devised. If even a small number of these institutions were global in scope, it would have an even more profound effect. Leaders of global organizations are true planetary citizens. Because their business units transcend national boundaries, their decisions affect not just economies, but societies – not just the direct concerns of business, but global issues of poverty, the environment, and security. These rising Stage IV executives and their organizations constitute an economic network whose operating philosophy can bind the planet in a common destiny.

In addition to the incipient rise of the Stage IV organization, there is another phenomenon occurring: the rise of the citizen groups, social entrepreneurs, and independent-sector organizations (nongovernmental organizations). Each one carries a different label, but they are all connected by a common motivation to represent the voices not accounted for otherwise. These elements of society, if developed properly, can embody the movement toward a Stage IV global civic society required to complement the work of the Stage IV institutions of commerce.

EPILOGUE

ANY THOUGHTS ABOUT ULTIMATE REALITY ARE
BOUND TO BE LIMITED, EVEN IF TRUE.

In the opening pages of this book, I gave a detailed description of
my inner experience of the Waco tornado, when I first had access to the
Source – even though I was a complete novice at the time and had no
idea what was happening or what "the Source" was. The events of the
search-and-rescue align with the classic description of operating from
that deeper place of knowing – acting without conscious awareness or
control, performing exceedingly difficult tasks without the sense of doing
so personally.

But what led me to leave my dorm room in the first place? Without
really thinking, I put on my windbreaker and ventured out. I did not
make a deliberate decision to go. I found myself heading in the direction
of downtown without assessing the risk of walking among all the live
electrical lines strewn across the streets. There was no one else on the
streets – yet the thought of hesitating never occurred to me.

Similarly, in the auditorium at the Shell Learning Center, at the very
instant that I heard the remarks of the Texaco chief operating officer,
my energy completely shifted, as if an internal rheostat had been turned
up to the maximum. I had an utter lack of self-concern, a fearlessness, a
sense of complete freedom. I didn't fully understand why, but nothing else
mattered to me but to follow that opening.

It was the same story in my office in Boston when I was walking out
the door and picked up *Fast Company*. It was ten-thirty at night, and I was
dead tired. I had put in a fourteen-hour day and was heading home to fall
into bed. What possessed me to pick up that magazine when I was halfway

out the door? And how is it that I opened the magazine to the exact page where Brian Arthur's interview appeared?

I've often thought of those events and about my insistence on talking with Brian. But for those moments in which I acted without conscious thought or control, we would never have met him, never have had the interview, and never have experienced the moment in the parking lot where Otto first placed Brian's coordinates around the drawing of a "U." Then there was Brian's uncharacteristic "instruction" to me to come to Baja and my response to him in the face of a full calendar. But for this entire sequence of events, I would not have had the encounter with the whales, there would never have been a Global Leadership Initiative, and there would never have been the Demonstration Projects, which positively affected thousands of lives.

When *Synchronicity* was written, even though I was just a beginner, I was learning how to move with the unfolding order, operating from what I then called "the implicate order," using the term I'd learned from David Bohm. My sense of identity had shifted, and I was beginning to see myself as part of the unfolding generative order. All I had to do was my work, treating it as my ultimate concern, then simply wait expectantly in the "warrior repose" with acute awareness for the opportune moment – the "cubic centimeter of chance." When the opportunity presented itself, I was required to move instantly without conscious premeditation.

I didn't really understand the moves I made in this state until much later. But I observed that very slight, deft movements at just the right time and place would have enormous consequences. Timing was crucial. When that moment came, with just the slightest gesture, all sorts of actions and results were brought into being.

This kind of effective action embodies the principle of economy of means, which is in evidence more and more as we learn to operate with real mastery in life. And this capacity is available to us all. As Francisco Varela said to me, this capacity is part of the natural order. It is the greatest of all human treasures.

━┥◆┝━○━┥◆┝━

At the end of my second Sacred Passage in Baja, all of us who had spent the previous week on solo gathered under the palapa to hear John

Milton address us on the subject of Source. John drew on his decades of training with Tibetan Buddhist and Taoist masters. At one point, he told us that he referred to the Source as "the Great Mystery." Then he paused for a moment, and I asked, "John, what's the difference between God and Source?"

John reflected for just a moment, and with an almost imperceptible smile replied, "Joseph, there's a thin line between the two. At a later time, we can talk about it."

Eighteen months later, I called him and said, "John, I'm about to finish this manuscript about the Source. Now is the time to talk to me about that thin line!"

So we set up a date for a telephone visit during which we spent a wonderful three hours together, going over everything he had taught me about the Source. I had made my own promise to myself that I would try to respond to this question, no matter how difficult it might be.

First, John reiterated something he had taught me long ago: "This is the fundamental truth. All forms are interconnected, constantly change, and continuously arise from and return to primordial Source." He continued, "Source is realized as the underlying reality out of which all form, including you yourself, manifests. This primordial unconditioned state is formless, yet gives birth to all form, holds all form, and is the ultimate receptacle for the dissolution of all form. Because no term can really describe it, I often simply point to it by calling it the Great Mystery."

As he spoke, I realized that John's definition of the Source is consistent with those I had learned from Bohm, Jahn, Dunne, and the Pari scientists. (After the call, I went back to look at David Peat's description of the Source, and John's words seemed to track what David had said, too.) John reconfirmed what Bob Jahn and David Peat had said to me: "When we connect to Source, we do so by means of a two-way dialogue. It's an activity *with* Source. We participate in the unfolding of form."

John said that everyone has access to Source. The capacity to connect to Source is "an enduring truth." There is no one religion or specific belief system that grants access to this realm. There is, John said, "a pathway to understanding the phenomenon of accessing Source individually or collectively that is independent of the ancient spiritual teachings. That way is through science, as you have learned, Joseph. Source can become active in your life, and you can participate with Source if you are willing to do the work to become adequate to do so. Anyone can participate in this unfolding, if they are willing to do the work to remove the filters and barriers that have been inculcated into us. This is available to us all."

Toward the end of our conversation, I pressed John again about whether God and Source were one and the same. His answer was highly surprising to me.

In John's view the Source is so fundamental that it is not incorrect to say that God arises from Source. John said, "Source existed before God; God, the Buddha, Krishna . . . all emanated from Source."

I tried to understand what John had said as best I could. What I came up with was similar to the way a Vedantic teacher in one of the Upanishads answered a student who had asked him to describe God. He said that the only way you can talk about God is to say "*Neti, neti*" – neither this, nor that.

"God" is the name we give as a kind of personification to the all-powerful creator. Without the sense of another being to talk to, it's difficult for us to pray or relate to the Source in any kind of personal way. The ultimate reality is beyond our ability to conceive it; and thus, it is so far beyond our *conception* of God that in the spirit of humility, we have to acknowledge that every time our human brains think of the traditional Judeo-Christian God, we are necessarily limiting the Source – we aren't saying "Krishna," for example. Since everything arises from the infinite potential of the Source, Krishna, like God, is potentially there and in a powerful way for some believers. In this way, all great spiritual traditions, including our Judeo-Christian idea of God, emerged from the Source: Hinduism, Christianity, Taoism, Buddhism, Judaism, Islam, and the indigenous traditions. Religion is a way of linking back to the Source through our own, limited human and cultural conceptions of truth or God.

Some theologians prefer Paul Tillich's more abstract term *Ground of Being* to the cultural associations that inevitably cling to the word "God." "Ground of Being" sounds a lot like "the Source." So I guess if the Ground of Being is one's idea of God, then Source and God might be two words for the same thing – or, as John said, separated by a "thin line." Still, any *thoughts* about ultimate reality are bound to be limited, even if true. The experience is beyond words. As Lao Tzu said, "The Tao that can be expressed in words is not the unchangeable Tao."

Initially, I wondered whether I should write about this dialogue with John. My hesitancy came from the fact that although John's view seemed plausible and consistent with all I had learned over the years, it was so radical that I felt uncertain about sharing it. But remembering all the radical scientific ideas I've shared in this book, I decided to share this spiritual idea as well, leaving the door open for readers to come to their own conclusions.

> We dance round in a ring and suppose,
> But the Secret sits in the middle and knows.

NOTES

page vi   From a wood engraving that first appeared in Camille Flammarion's *L'atmosphère: météorologie populaire* (1888).

INTRODUCTION
page 1   Introduction by Peter Senge (San Francisco: Berrett-Koehler, 1996).

page 2   H. D. Brown and W. Wiegand, "Cosmic Law – Patterns in the Universe" in *The FMBR – Where Science and Consciousness Produce Wisdom* 23 Nov. 2010, www.fmbr.org/cosmiclaw/index.htm.

page 2   In conversation with the author, London, 28 July 1980.

page 3   "Sensors, Filters, and the Source of Reality," in *The Pertinence of the Princeton Engineering Anomalies Research (PEAR) Laboratory to the Pursuit of Global Health*, special issue of *Explore: the Journal of Science and Healing* 3, no. 3 (May/June, 2007), 326.

page 3   Eleanor Rosch, "'Spit Straight Up – Learn Something!': Can Tibetan Buddhism Inform the Cognitive Sciences?" unpublished manuscript, 2.

page 3   With Peter Senge, C. Otto Scharmer, and Betty Sue Flowers (NY: Doubleday, 2005).

page 4   Robert Greenleaf, *The Servant as Leader* (Newton Center, MA: Robert K. Greenleaf Center, 1973 [1970]).

page 4   M. Scott Peck, *The Different Drum*, (New York: Touchstone [Simon & Schuster], 1988),187.

PROLOGUE
page 7   In conversation with the author in London on 28 July 1980.

3. BIRTH OF THE U-THEORY
page 18   Conversation with W. Brian Arthur, Xerox PARC, Palo Alto, CA: Joseph Jaworski, Gary Jusela, C. Otto Scharmer, 16 April 1999.

4. A LABORATORY FOR CREATIVE DISCOVERY
page 22   Jaworski and Scharmer, *Leadership in the New Economy: Sensing and Actualizing Emerging Futures* (Beverly, MA: Generon Consulting and Cambridge, MA: Society for Organizational Learning, Cambridge MA.), 2000. (Text is available at www.generoninternational.com.)

5. THE RED BOOK

page 26   NY and Oxford: Oxford University Press.

page 27   Boston: MIT Press, 1992.

page 27   "'Spit Straight Up – Learn Something!': Can Tibetan Buddhism Inform the Cognitive Sciences?" unpublished manuscript, 2.

7. DEMONSTRATION PROJECTS

page 37   "About the Meadowlark Project," at www.meadowlarkinstitute.org.

page 37   From material given to Generon by the coalition of leaders.

page 38   At www.meadowlarkinstitute.org.

page 38   Meadowlark Institute home page, www.meadowlarkinstitute.org.

9. LEARNING HARD LESSONS

page 44   Reprinted with permission from Robert Rabbin.

10. ENCOUNTER IN THE NETHERLANDS

page 50   Jaworski and Scharmer, *Leadership in the New Economy*, op. cit., 8.

page 50   A description of the U-Procedure was published in 1975 in the Netherlands by Friedrich Glasl and Leo de la Houssaye, *Organisatie-ontwikkeling in de praktijk* (Brussels/Amsterdam: Elsevier). At the same time a German translation was published under the title *Organisationsentwicklung* (Bern/ Stuttgart: Haupt Verlag). An English translation of the U-Procedure was first published in Friedrich Glasl, *The Enterprise of the Future* (Gloucester: Hawthorn Press, 1997), 67.

page 50   *Man on the Threshold: The Challenge of Inner Development* (Stroud, UK: Hawthorn Press, 1990).

page 50   Trans. H. S. Lake (London: Rudolf Steiner Press, 1993).

page 51   Oxford: Blackwells, 1990 [1969]. Later, Glasl and Lievegoed together published a new and expanded German version, *Dynamische Unternehmensentwicklung* (Bern/Stuttgart/Wien: Haupt Verlag, 1993).

page 51   Stroud, UK: Hawthorn Press, 1997.

11. STAGE IV LEADERS

page 53   *The Road Less Traveled: A New Psychology of Love, Traditional Values, and Spiritual Growth* (New York: Touchstone/Simon & Schuster, 1988 [1978]).

page 53   New York: Touchstone / Simon & Schuster, 1998 [1987]).

page 53   *Using the Everyday Challenges of Business to Transform Businesses and Organizations* (London: Godsfield Press, 2003).

13. JOURNEY TO PARI

page 61   D. Bohm and F. D. Peat, *Science, Order and Creativity* (Toronto and New York: Bantam Books), 1987.

page 61   Ibid.

page 61   London: Routledge & Kegan Paul, 1980.

page 62   The story of the founding of the American Leadership Forum, including the original meeting with Bohm, is told in my book, *Synchronicity* (San Francisco: Berrett-Koehler, 1996).

page 65   F. David Peat, *Infinite Potential: The Life and Times of David Bohm* (Reading, MA, and New York: Addison Wesley/Helix Books, 1996), 193.

page 65   Henri Bortoft, *The Wholeness of Nature: Goethe's Way towards a Science of Conscious Participation in Nature* (Aurora, CO: Lindisfarne Press, 1996).

page 66   *Changing Consciousness: Exploring the Hidden Source of the Social, Political, and Environmental Crises Facing Our World* (New York: Harper Collins, 1991).

14. THE FINITE, THE INFINITE, AND THE DESTINY STATE

page 67   Peat, *Infinite Potential*, 322.

page 67   Ibid.

15. NONLOCALITY AND THE IMPLICATE ORDER

page 71   Conversation with the author, London, 1980.

page 71   Quoted by Gary Zukav, *The Dancing Wu Li Masters: An Overview of the New Physics* (New York: Bantam New Age Books, 1980 [1979]), 299.

page 72   Peat, *Infinite Potential*, 263.

page 72   London conversation with Bohm; see also *Synchronicity*, 174.

page 73   Peat, *Infinite Potential*, 264.

page 73   Ibid., 265.

page 73   Peat, *Infinite Potential*, 301.

page 74   Ibid., 297.

page 74   Ibid., 297.

page 74   Ibid., 298.

16. INDIGENOUS SCIENCE

page 78   *Blackfoot Physics: A Journey into the Native American Universe* (Boston, MA: Weisner Books), 2002.

page 80   These quotes and the following story are taken from a recorded transcript of a workshop in Lahaska, PA (May 2008); used with the kind permission of Lynne Twist.

17. THE INNER STATE

page 85   London: Routledge, 1994.

page 86   In this section, I am capitalizing the world "Dialogue" to connote "Bohmian Dialogue" and differentiate it from ordinary dialogue.

page 86   Peter Senge, *The Fifth Discipline* (NY: Currency / Doubleday, rev. ed. 2006 [1990]).

page 87   This booklet has subsequently been revised, extended, and incorporated into a more comprehensive volume by the same name. See D. Bohm, *On Dialogue* (London: Routledge, 1996).

page 89   I'm indebted to Lee for sending me his manuscript of an essay that later appeared as "Wholeness Regained: Revisiting Bohm's Dialogue" in Bela Banathy and Patrick Jenlink, eds., *Dialogue as a Means of Collective Communication* (New York: Kluwer-Plenam Academic Publishing, 2004).

18. ENCOUNTERING THE AUTHENTIC WHOLE

page 91   *Synchronicity: The Bridge between Matter and Mind*, (Toronto and New York: Bantam Books, 1987), 233.

page 92   Bortoft, *The Wholeness of Nature*, 81.

page 92   Op. cit., 233.

page 93   See *Presence*, 45–48.

page 93   Conversation with W. Brian Arthur, Xerox PARC, Palo Alto, CA, April 16, 1999.

19. PARTNERS IN EVOLUTION

page 95   Donald Factor, ed., *Unfolding Meaning: A Weekend of Dialogue of David Bohm* (Mickleton, England: Foundation House Publishers, 1985).

page 96   "Meaning as Being in the Implicate Order Philosophy of David Bohm: A Conversation," in D. J. Hiley and D. Peat, eds., *Quantum Implications*, 436–50.

page 96   Ibid., 439.

page 96   Ibid.,450.

page 96   Peat, *Synchronicity*, 233.

20. SCIENCE AND HUMAN POSSIBILITY

page 97   "I'm Not Looking, Honest", *The Economist*, (March 5, 2009) www.economist.com/node/13226725?story_id=13226725.

page 101   *Dogs That Know When Their Owners Are Coming Home: And Other Unexplained Powers of Animals* (New York: Three Rivers Press/Random House, 2000 [1999]).

21. REMOTE VIEWING

page 103   In the late 1970s, SRI became an independent research organization known as SRI International.

page 104   See D. Radin, *The Conscious Universe* (New York: Harper, 1997),101.

page 104   C. M. Bache, *The Living Classroom: Teaching and Collective Consciousness* (New York and Albany: SUNY Press, 2008), 76; quoting B. J. Dunne and R. G. Jahn, "Information and Uncertainty in Remote Perception Research," *Journal of Scientific Exploration* 17, no. 2 (2003),207–41.

22. THE POWERFUL NATURE OF HUMAN INTENTION

page 110   *The Pertinence of the Princeton Engineering Anomalies Research (PEAR) Laboratory to the Pursuit of Global Health*, op. cit.

page 110 "PEAR Lab and Nonlocal Mind: Why They Matter," 191–96.

page 111 New York: HarperOne/HarperCollins, 1997 [1993].

page 112 D. Radin, *Conscious Universe*, 140. According to Radin, a more recent meta-analysis of the REG data from 1959–2000 showed a similar result. See Radin and Nelson, "Evidence for Consciousness-Related Anomalies in Random Physical Systems" 19, no. 12 *Foundation of Physics* (1989), 1499–514.

page 112 "PEAR Lab and Nonlocal Mind: Why They Matter," 326.

23. COLLECTIVE COHERENCE

page 113 D. Radin, *Entangled Minds: Extrasensory Experiences in a Quantum Reality* (NY: Paraview Pocket Books/Simon & Shuster, 2006), 198.

page 113 *The Conscious Universe: The Scientific Truth of Psychic Phenomena* (New York: HarperOne/HarperCollins, 1997).

page 114 R. D. Nelson, D.I. Radin, R. Shoup, and P. Bancle, "Correlation of Continuous Random Data with Major World Events," *Foundation of Physics Letter* 15, no. 6 (2000), 537–50. I am indebted to Christopher M. Bache for his extremely well-written summary of the current scientific research on psychic phenomena and collective consciousness, *The Living Classroom*, op. cit. See, particularly, pages 79–83 on animal consciousness and pages 86–90 on the Global Consciousness Project.

page 114 Radin, *Entangled Minds*, 198.

page 115 R. D. Nelson, *Terrorist Disaster: September 11, 2001*, http://noosphere.princeton.edu/williams/GCP911.html (2002).

24. THE SOURCE OF REALITY

page 117 In conversation with the author in Pari. See also Peat, *Synchronicity*, 195.

page 118 The first five of these principles are reflected in R. G. Jahn and B.J. Dunne, op. cit., 326–37; the sixth was added in conversation with the author.

page 119 M. Buber, *I and Thou* (NY: Charles Scribner's Sons, 1970 [1923]).

page 120 "Sensors, Filters, and the Source of Reality," 336.

25. FORESIGHT

page 123 In conversation with the author, November 2008.

page 123 R.K. Greenleaf, *Servant Leadership: A Journey into the Nature of Legitimate Power and Greatness* (NY: Paulist Press, 1977), 21–22.

page 123 Quoted in: "Is This REALLY Proof that Man Can See into the Future?" (London: *Daily Mail*, May 4, 2007), www.dailymail.co.uk/sciencetech/article-452833/Is-REALLY-proof-man-future.html. Accessed 1 June 2011.

page 124 D. Radin, *Entangled Minds*, 179.

page 124 *The Power of Premonitions: How Knowing the Future Can Shape Our Lives* (New York: Dutton Penguin Group, 2003), 203.

page 124 Dossey, ibid., 63.

page 124 Ibid., 64.

page 125   Ibid., 63.

page 125   See also Dossey, ibid., 72.

page 125   Ibid., 74.

26. ACCESSING THE SOURCE – THE SURPRISING ROLE OF THE HEART

page 127   www.goodreads.com/quotes/show/7090.

page 128   See Jaworski and Scharmer, *Leadership in the New Economy*, op. cit., 28.

page 128   See also Childre and Cryer, *From Chaos to Coherence* (Boulder Creek, CA: Planetary, 2000), 53–58.

page 129   Jaworski and Scharmer, *Leadership in the New Economy*, op. cit., 28.

page 129   From a recorded transcript of a workshop in Lahaska, PA (May 2008).

page 129   R. McCraty, M. Atkinson, and R. T. Bradley, "Electrophysiological Evidence of Intuition: Part 1. The Surprising Role of the Heart." *Journal of Alternative and Complimentary Medicine* 10 (2004), 133–43.

page 130   Ibid., 142.

page 130   Ibid., 143.

page 130   McCraty et al., "Electrophysiological Evidence of Intuition: Part 2. A System-wide Process?" *Journal of Alternative and Complementary Medicine*, 10 (2004), 334.

27. GROUP ENTRAINMENT

page 133   From a recorded transcript of a workshop in Lahaska, PA (May 2008).

page 134   See also Childre and Cyer, *From Chaos to Coherence*, op. cit., 14, 201–202.

page 134   Workshop transcript.

28. THE POWER OF PASSIONATE ATTENTION

page 135   R.T. Bradley, R. McCraty, M. Atkinson, and M. Gillin, "Nonlocal Intuition in Entrepreneurs and Non-Entrepreneurs: An Experiential Comparison Using Electrophysiological Measures," forthcoming in *Regional Frontiers of Entrepreneurial Research*, ms., 3.

page 135   Ibid., 12.

page 136   Ibid., 4

page 136   Ibid., 3.

29. CONNECTING TO THE SOURCE

page 139   Scott Peck, "The Frontier of Group Space," introduction to Gozdz, ed., *Community Building: Renewing Spirit and Learning in Business* (San Francisco: New Leaders Press, Sterling & Stone, Inc., 1995), 2.

page 139   www.generoninternational.com.

page 140   See www.generoninternational.com.

page 141   Chicago: U of Chicago Press, 2009 [1966].

page 141   with Harry Prosch (Chicago: U of Chicago Press, 1977 [1975]).

page 141   Chicago: U of Chicago Press, 1974 [1958].

page 141   I am grateful to Amartya Sin for the insightful foreword to *The Tacit Dimension* that was first written for the 2009 republication. I have relied heavily on the content of this excellent foreword for the background information on Polanyi.

page 142   *Personal Knowledge*, 64.

page 142   Ibid., 87.

page 142   Ibid., 285.

page 142   Ibid,. 405.

page 142   *The Tacit Dimension*, 89.

30. THE STRUCTURE OF KNOWLEDGE CREATION

page 143   Ibid.

page 144   *Personal Knowledge*, 123.

page 144   Ibid., 64.

page 144   Ibid., 88.

page 144   Polanyi and Prosch, *Meaning*, op. cit., 194.

page 145   Ibid., 157.

page 145   Ibid., 96.

page 145   Ibid., 157

page 145   *Personal Knowledge*, 143.

page 146   Ibid., 130.

31. THE RELEASE OF LIMITING BELIEF SYSTEMS

page 147   In conversation with the author at Shell Centre, London, June 1990.

page 147   Brown and Wiegand, op. cit.

32. SUDDEN ILLUMINATION

page 149   Allan L. Combs, *Radiance of Being: Complexity, Chaos and the Evolution of Consciousness* (St. Paul, Minnesota: Paragon House, 1995), p. 156.

page 149   Brown and Wiegand, op. cit. Dean Brown served as a mentor to my partner, Kazmierz Gozdz for many years. Brown had a profound influence on Kaz's thought and his understanding of the universe. Kaz introduced me to *Cosmic Law* and helped me to understand its contents. I found the work fascinating and was able to navigate its depths largely due to Kaz's guidance.

page 149   Senge, *The Fifth Discipline*, 13.

page 149   Brown and Wiegand, *Cosmic Law*, 31.

page 150   Ibid., 32.

page 150   Private conversation at the Dulany Ranch, Centennial Valley, MT.

page 150   T. A. Edison quoted in N. Baldwin, *Edison: Inventing the Century* (New York: Hyperion, 1995), 376.

page 150   Combs, *Radiance of Being*, 156.

page 151   Ibid., 156.

page 151   Ibid., 157.

33. ANCIENT ANTECEDENTS

page 153   C. Otto Scharmer, "Conversation with Eleanor Rosch: Primary Knowing: When Perception Arises from the Whole Field," (Interview, October 15, 1999).

page 153   Pages 185–213.

page 154   Scharmer, "Conversation with Eleanor Rosch," op. cit., n.p.

page 154   New York: Doubleday/Dolphin, 1986. I am deeply grateful to Mr. Wing for this translation. I have relied heavily on his "Notes on the Translation" and his Introduction to the book, pages 10–16, for the whole of this chapter.

page 154   Quoted in Wing, *The Tao of Power*, 9.

page 155   Wing, 15.

page 155   Ibid., 15.

34. NATURE AND SACRED SPACES

page 158   I have not been able to locate the source of this quotation.

page 158   "Self-realization is born and matures in a distinctive kind of awareness, an awareness that has been described in many different ways by many different people. . . . Perception of the miraculous is the subjective essence of self-realization, the root from which man's highest features and experiences grow." Michael Stark and Michael Washburn, "Beyond the Norm: A Speculative Model of Self Realization," *Journal of Religion and Health* 16, no. 1 (1977), 58–59.

35. THE POWER OF LOVE

page 161   http://thinkexist.com/quotation/someday-after_mastering_the_winds-the_waves-the/218170.html

page 161   *Quantum Implications*, 450. Also, conversations with Nichol, Hiley, and Peat in Pari.

page 162   L. de Broglie, "The Role of the Engineer in the Age of Science," *New Perspectives in Physics*, trans. A. J. Pomerans (New York: Basic Books, 1962), 231.

page 162   http://thinkexist.com/quotation/someday-after_mastering_the_winds-the_waves-the/218170.html

36. A DISCIPLINED PATH

page 163   Conversation with author, Baja, Mexico, February 2008.

page 163   As reported to me by Lee Nichol.

page 163   Polanyi and Prosch, *Meaning*, 129.

page 166 These are the words of John Kabat-Zinn, whom we interviewed in 1999 as a part of the Alliance research project. At that time, Dr. Kabat-Zinn was the executive director of the Center of Mindfulness in Meditation, Healthcare and Society at the University of Massachusetts Medical Center. Dr. Kabat-Zinn's books on mindfulness meditation are best sellers, and he is considered to be one of the foremost authorities in the field. I highly recommend his books and DVDs as a first step into the practice.

page 166 A DVD series available through www.sacredpassage.com.

page 166 With a foreword by Larry Dossey (New York: Ballantine Books, 1997).

page 167 Ibid., 273.

page 168 Peat, *Synchronicity*, 182.

37. DEVELOPING STAGE IV LEADERSHIP

page 169 *The Perennial Philosophy* (New York: Harper & Brothers, 1945), vii.

page 170 Ibid.

page 170 Ibid.

page 170 Ibid., vii–ix.

page 171 For a record of Admiral Stockdale's speeches and essays, see *A Vietnam Experience: Ten Years of Reflections* (Palo Alto, CA: Hoover Press Publications, 1984).

page 172 A *Vietnam Experience*, 121.

page 172 Ibid., 70.

page 173 Ibid., 130.

page 173 Ibid., 10.

page 173 Ibid., 32.

page 173 Ibid., 118.

page 174 Jim and Sybil Stockdale, *In Love and War* (New York: Harper & Row, 1984), 202.

38. SCAFFOLDING STAGE IV ORGANIZATIONS

page 177 See Laura E. Berk and Adam Winsler, *Scaffolding Children's Learning: Vygotsky and Early Childhood Education* (Washington, DC: National Association for the Education of Young Children, 1955).

page 177 Kaz Gozdz first introduced this practice in 1999 in the Decurion Corporation, an emerging Stage IV organization.

page 178 These seven practices were formulated by Kaz Gozdz and the author in 2010 and first introduced at a public workshop in Vaught, Netherlands, in May of that year.

page 181 Polanyi and Prosch, *Meaning*, op. cit., 194.

39. STAGE IV ENTERPRISES: TWO STORIES

page 184   *Presence,* 141–42.

page 185   "Near-Death Experience, Consciousness and the Brain: A New Concept about the Continuity of Our Consciousness Based on Recent Scientific Research on Near-Death Experience in Survivors of Cardiac Arrest," later published as *Consciousness beyond Life: The Science of Near-Death Experience* (New York: HarperOne, 2010).

page 185   Manuscript cited, n.p.

page 185   Ibid., n.p.

page 187   Details of this story were taken from a transcript of a workshop recording, May 2008. Some elements of this story also appear in Senge's *Fifth Discipline* and in an essay by Marsing entitled, "How to 'Walk the Talk' without Falling off a Cliff" in Peter Senge, et al., *The Dance of Change: The Challenges to Sustaining Momentum in Learning Organizations* (New York: Doubleday, 1999), 214–20.

EPILOGUE

page 199   Robert Frost, "The Secret Sits," *The Poetry of Robert Frost,* Edward C. Lathem, ed. (New York: Holt, Rinehart and Winston, 1969 [1942]), 362. Copyright © 1969 Henry Holt & Co. Reprinted by arrangement with Henry Holt & Co.

ACKNOWLEDGMENTS

This book chronicles a journey that spans fifteen years, beginning after the completion of my first book, *Synchronicity: The Inner Path of Leadership*. Along the way, I continued to meet the most remarkable people who added important new dimensions to my life and to my understanding of the capacity we have to sense and actualize emerging futures and to shape the future instead of simply responding to the forces at large. Many of these remarkable people are mentioned among the pages of this book, but others are not. To all of them, I express my heartfelt gratitude.

I owe an additional debt of gratitude:

- To my business partner, Susan M. Taylor, for the consistent and unwavering support she gave to me from the moment I decided to write this book. I say this literally: but for her support, her care, and attention to the project all along the way, this book would not exist today. She has devoted over four years of her life-energy to helping me in every phase of the work. She encouraged me to begin the project, served as Director of Research, and provided encouragement, support, and invaluable advice as a thinking partner.

- To Betty Sue Flowers for her exceedingly high competence in acting as my editor and collaborator. Her experience as a member of my team of scenario planners at the Royal Dutch Shell Group of companies and her work with me on both editions of *Synchronicity* provided the foundation needed for her extraordinary contribution to this work.

- To my dear friend and distinguished colleague W. Brian Arthur, who has served Generon and me as guide and teacher for over thirteen years.

- To my friend John P. Milton, who has acted as my trusted guide and mentor all these years.

- To my business partner, Kazimierz Gozdz, for his vigorous and intelligent support during the final phase of writing the manuscript and for sharing with me the product of two decades of his work in the field of community building, transpersonal psychology, and organizational development.

- To Arthur Klebanoff of Scott Meredith Agency, my friend of over thirty years, who provided intellectual and moral support at every stage.

- To Steve Piersanti and his team at Berrett-Koehler for all their hard work and good suggestions.

- And, finally, to Deborah A. Moore, for her usual high competence in preparation of the manuscript.

INDEX

Joseph Jaworski   Photo © Sigrid Estrada

ABOUT THE AUTHOR

Joseph began his professional career at Bracewell and Patterson (now Bracewell and Giuliani), a prominent international law firm, where he was a senior partner and member of the Executive Committee. He gained early success as a courtroom lawyer using intuitive methods for preparation of his cases, including interviewing and cross-examining witnesses and presenting to juries, that he was unable to explain. He had no language for describing those methodologies or any way to codify them. The knowledge was tacit to him.

This knowledge was gained in his early years by observing his father, who was one of the most respected trial lawyers in the country, the former World War II war crimes prosecutor and Watergate prosecutor, Leon Jaworski. Joseph knew him as "the Colonel" because this is the way all of

his father's partners and young associates at his father's law firm referred
to him.

From his earliest years, Joseph observed his father spending time
in nature – first in the gardens of his home and later, after the war, at
his ranch in the Texas hill country. The Colonel always carried a small
notebook or scrap of paper in his shirt pocket, making notes to himself
as ideas, new revelations, and intuitions would come to him. He used the
same process when he woke up with an idea during the night. In later
years, the Colonel told Joseph that he would awake from his dreamlike
state (particularly when he was in trial or preparing for trial) and would
jot down insights he had gained in this state. Joseph also observed how
the Colonel conducted himself during close encounters with associates
and people with whom he was conducting business. There seemed to be
a special connection between the Colonel and those with whom he was
communicating – a kind of connection Joseph could not put his finger on,
but which was palpable to him.

Finally, Joseph noted there was a sense of destiny that his father
possessed. It was never spoken about, but it was always there. For
example, the Colonel had a close relationship with Lyndon B. Johnson,
one that began years before Johnson ascended to the office of President of
the United States. During his first term of office, after President Kennedy
was assassinated, President Johnson offered the Colonel an appointment
at the United States Supreme Court. The day before the Colonel
declined, he told Joseph, then a young lawyer, "Bud, I can't exactly put
my finger on it, but I *know* I should not accept this position. It would
limit my capacity to serve my country later. I know there is more for me
to do." But for that decision, the Colonel would not have been available
to serve as the Watergate special prosecutor during the country's most
grave Constitutional crisis.

Using the tacit knowledge learned from his father and from his direct
experiences over the years, Joseph began to consistently produce results
exceeding customary norms in the worlds of law, entrepreneurship,
strategic planning, and organizational transformation. In 1975, in his first
year of eligibility, Joseph was elected as a Fellow of the American College
of Trial Lawyers, an honor awarded to the top one percent of American
litigators. He also helped found several highly successful businesses,

including a life insurance company and an oil refining company. In addition, he founded and ran a quarter horse breeding operation (Circle J Enterprises) that in 1972 produced an American Quarter Horse Supreme Champion, then only the sixteenth such champion in the history of the breed.

An example of the kind of intuitive knowledge that Joseph acted on occurred when he was working cattle with a ranch hand who expressed an interest in sculpting but was too far in debt to take time from his day labors to begin. Sensing the possibility, Joseph gave the hand, Jim Reno, enough money to begin his career as an equine sculptor. By the third year, Reno's sculptures were selling for up to forty thousand dollars each, and in 1973 Reno was selected to create the monumental sculpture of the racing legend, Secretariat, that now stands at Belmont Park. By the time of his death in 2008, Reno was one of the most respected equine sculptors in America.

In 1980, Joseph founded the American Leadership Forum, a nongovernmental organization dedicated to strengthening collaborative civic leadership in the United States. Ten years later, he joined the Royal Dutch/Shell Group of companies in London to head Shell's renowned team of scenario planners. Under his leadership, the Shell team made a fundamental shift in the way the company framed and used scenarios as a tool for strategy formation. Joseph encouraged the company to use scenarios not merely to adapt to different possible futures, but to *generate* – to participate in bringing forth – better futures.

Joseph returned to the United States as a senior fellow and member of the Board of Governors of the MIT Center for Organizational Learning, later cofounding the Society for Organizational Learning (SoL). He is author of the international best-seller, *Synchronicity: The Inner Path of Leadership* and coauthor of *Presence: An Exploration of Profound Change in People, Organizations, and Society*, which explores the collaborative development of a new theory of profound innovation and change.

Joseph's older son, Joe, is the Mayor of Galveston and practices law in the Gulf Coast region of Texas. His younger children, Leon and Shannon, live in Minnesota and California, respectively. Joseph currently lives in Stowe, in the Green Mountains of Vermont.

GENERON INTERNATIONAL

Generon is an international consulting firm specializing in four distinct areas of practice:

- Advanced decision-making and strategy formation

- Innovation

- Enhanced human performance and operational excellence

- Fundamental institutional renewal

Our focus is on developing and sustaining Stage IV organizations led by Stage IV leaders – those who exhibit a capacity for extraordinary functioning and performance. At the heart of this quality of performance is the capacity for accessing tacit knowing, which can be used for breakthrough thinking, strategy formation, and innovation, including envisioning and creating the kind of institutions or society we desire.

Generon International
(802) 253–3080
www.generoninternational.com

Another Book by Joseph Jaworski

Synchronicity
The Inner Path of Leadership, Expanded Second Edition

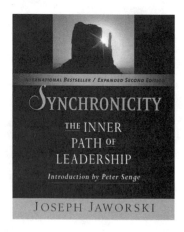

In this now-classic book, Joseph Jaworski shares the story of his journey
to a deeper understanding of leadership. Leadership, he discovered, has
more to do with our being—our total orientation of character and consciousness—than with what we do. He argues that understanding the
interconnectedness of all things and pursuing a deep commitment within
that understanding will enable us to consciously take advantage of what
Carl Jung called "synchronicity"—"a collaboration between persons and
events that seems to enlist the cooperation of fate." Jaworski examines
three fundamental shifts of mind that free us to experience synchronicity.
This long-awaited second edition includes excerpts from the hundreds of
letters Jaworski has received testifying to the profound impact of the book's
message and describes the first steps that eventually led to his discovery of
the four principles outlined in *Source*.

Paperback, 264 pages, ISBN 978-1-60994-017-1
PDF ebook, ISBN 978-1-60994-018-8

Berrett–Koehler Publishers, Inc.
www.bkconnection.com   **800.929.2929**

Berrett–Koehler
Publishers

Berrett-Koehler is an independent publisher dedicated to an ambitious mission: *Creating a World That Works for All*.

We believe that to truly create a better world, action is needed at all levels—individual, organizational, and societal. At the individual level, our publications help people align their lives with their values and with their aspirations for a better world. At the organizational level, our publications promote progressive leadership and management practices, socially responsible approaches to business, and humane and effective organizations. At the societal level, our publications advance social and economic justice, shared prosperity, sustainability, and new solutions to national and global issues.

A major theme of our publications is "Opening Up New Space." Berrett-Koehler titles challenge conventional thinking, introduce new ideas, and foster positive change. Their common quest is changing the underlying beliefs, mindsets, institutions, and structures that keep generating the same cycles of problems, no matter who our leaders are or what improvement programs we adopt.

We strive to practice what we preach—to operate our publishing company in line with the ideas in our books. At the core of our approach is stewardship, which we define as a deep sense of responsibility to administer the company for the benefit of all of our "stakeholder" groups: authors, customers, employees, investors, service providers, and the communities and environment around us.

We are grateful to the thousands of readers, authors, and other friends of the company who consider themselves to be part of the "BK Community." We hope that you, too, will join us in our mission.

A BK Business Book

This book is part of our BK Business series. BK Business titles pioneer new and progressive leadership and management practices in all types of public, private, and nonprofit organizations. They promote socially responsible approaches to business, innovative organizational change methods, and more humane and effective organizations.

Berrett–Koehler Publishers

A community dedicated to creating
a world that works for all

Visit Our Website: www.bkconnection.com

Read book excerpts, see author videos and Internet movies, read our authors' blogs, join discussion groups, download book apps, find out about the BK Affiliate Network, browse subject-area libraries of books, get special discounts, and more!

Subscribe to Our Free E-Newsletter, the *BK Communiqué*

Be the first to hear about new publications, special discount offers, exclusive articles, news about bestsellers, and more! Get on the list for our free e-newsletter by going to **www.bkconnection.com**.

Get Quantity Discounts

Berrett-Koehler books are available at quantity discounts for orders of ten or more copies. Please call us toll-free at (800) 929-2929 or email us at bkp .orders@aidcvt.com.

Join the BK Community

BKcommunity.com is a virtual meeting place where people from around the world can engage with kindred spirits to create a world that works for all. BKcommunity.com members may create their own profiles, blog, start and participate in forums and discussion groups, post photos and videos, answer surveys, announce and register for upcoming events, and chat with others online in real time. Please join the conversation!

Certified

Corporation
bcorporation.net